BOUQUETS WITH PERSONALITY

BOUQUETS WITH PERSONALITY

Lucinda Rooney

Photographs by Mick Hales

Stewart, Tabori & Chang
New York

Published in 2009 by Stewart, Tabori & Chang
An imprint of Abrams

Text copyright © 2009 Lucinda Rooney
Photographs copyright © 2009 Mick Hales

Library of Congress Cataloging-in-Publication Data:

Rooney, Lucinda.
  Bouquets with personality / Lucinda Rooney ; photographs by Mick Hales.
    p. cm.
  Includes bibliographical references and index.
  ISBN 978-1-58479-788-3 (alk. paper)
  Bouquets. I. Hales, Michael. II. Title.
SB449.5.B65R66 2009
745.92--dc22   2009000704

Editor: Denise Otis
Designer: Alissa Faden
Production Manager: Tina Cameron

The text of this book was composed in Democratica, Hoefler Text, and Today.

Printed and bound in China
10 9 8 7 6 5 4 3 2 1

THE ART OF BOOKS SINCE 1949
115 West 18th Street
New York, NY 10011
www.hnabooks.com

THIS BOOK IS DEDICATED TO MY GRANDMOTHER, CHOYCE WATERMAN

I was raised by my grandparents on a small farm in the foothills of the Adirondacks in upstate New York. My grandmother was a patient woman, very caring and affable, always willing to have me tag along when she was going to the garden. The flowers filled me with joy. I spent hours beside her on those long summer days, weeding and also gathering vegetables for dinner. She was a wonderful cook and would go to great lengths to collect special ingredients. For a summer dessert we would attack the raspberry patch, which stood off to the left of the main garden. In the hot afternoon sun we somehow withstood the prickly branches to get the sweet berries they produced. I must confess that more of what I picked went into my mouth than into my tin.

Flowers, gardens, and cooking made up my way of life with my grandmother. People said she had a green thumb. I believe a green thumb comes from a giving heart. I spent all my summers with her on the farm until I was fourteen.

The gardens would be laid to rest that year, but like every good gardener my grandmother left me a gift: seeds to plant . . .

CONTENTS

INTRODUCTION

SOURCES AND SUPPLIERS

INDEX

"Go confidently in the direction of your dreams. Live the life you have imagined."

INTRODUCTION

For years this exhortation adapted from Henry David Thoreau was taped to the dashboard of my car so that I would be reminded never to give up on my dreams. Flowers found their way into my life at a very early age, and I was certain that one day I would find my own path and that at some point I would be able to share my love for gardens, flowers, and the joys of life. A most amazing journey would lie ahead of me, filled with unexpected triumphs and trials that have helped me to become more of who I am.

As a young artist I found my way to Vermont, and my very first job was as Maria Von Trapp's housekeeper at her home and inn in Stowe. I think my long blond hair and fitted dirndl gave me an Austrian look and helped me to secure the position! Maria was an inspiration to me, as she loved flowers. The interior windowsills of the inn were a profusion of plants and flowers, and summer gardens enriched the already enchanting landscape. I would go on to wait tables at many fine restaurants in Vermont, and there, too, I would find myself decorating the tables with flowers.

Ten years later some dreams turned to realities and I went to study at the Royal Botanic Gardens, Kew. There I came to understand the true essence of flowers. After arriving home from England I opened a business designing flowers for weddings: the groundwork for my future. One thing led to another and before I knew it I was designing and styling flowers for national magazines, fashion shoots, and television commercials.

The concept for this book, *Bouquets with Personality,* really came to me by accident several years ago. When I was asked to lecture at the Boston Flower Show for the second time, I was unsure what to lecture about. The previous year I had given a slide show and talk about some flower projects I had worked on for films and advertising. I'm afraid I was met with an audience of just twelve, whose unresponsiveness left me feeling somewhat intimidated. So when I was asked to lecture the next year, I was determined to find some way to engage the audience. Since people do love flowers, I decided to arrive with a lot of flowers and see if I could stand up and design something that would interest them. Realizing that I design by relating the personalities of flowers to the personalities of people, I called the lecture "Bouquets with Personality."

There were perhaps thirty people present, and, nervously, I began to design my first bouquet, which I referred to as a bouquet of harmony. The audience showed some interest, and it occurred to me to bring people up on stage and interact with them as I designed bouquets to resemble their personalities. The first person I brought up was a lovely young lady about the age of eight. Weaving together flowers in shades of whites and greens and explaining what the flowers were and why I was choosing them, I created a bouquet to complement her gentle nature. I proceeded to give her the bouquet and she accepted it with delight and enthusiasm. From there I relaxed into the rest of the evening. Thinking I had never designed a bouquet for a man, I asked for a volunteer. An elderly gentleman from the audience eagerly participated and I designed a vibrant bouquet of lilacs and roses in strong colors of purple and orange. When I handed it to him, I asked if

> Arranging flowers is a delightful and sometimes humorous process. It is much easier to comprehend when you can relate it to something you know and understand: the personalities of people.

he was going to give this bouquet to his wife. He quickly answered, "No, nobody has ever done this for me before. I will keep it for myself."

Feeling more confident, I proceeded to design what I referred to as my Type A personality bouquet. This one went over particularly well. A young man and his wife joined me on stage. He referred to his wife as the one with the Type A personality. When I completed the arrangement I handed it to the husband so that he could see how beautiful a Type A personality can be. I ended up with a standing room only audience. For one hour I designed with all my heart and my concept was validated.

Arranging flowers is a delightful and sometimes humorous process. It is much easier to comprehend when you can relate it to something you know and understand: the personalities of people. With this in mind I began teaching at the New York Botanical Gardens in the Bronx and at Longwood Gardens in Kennett Square, Pennsylvania. I respect the more formal floral design classes and their procedures. There is a great deal to be gleaned from them. My ideas and techniques are not meant to diminish their value but to encourage people to have fun when designing with flowers. Flowers always have something to say, even in the simplest displays. Sometimes the most unusual and interesting arrangements I have put together came straight from the garden without much prior thought.

I tell my students that when you are putting flowers together, think of them just as though you were forming a committee of different personalities. When we work too hard at trying to design with flowers, the results show it. Sometimes I see students grip the flowers so hard that they seem to squeeze the very life out of them. Relax, I tell them, if you are unhappy with the results you can always take your arrangement apart and start again.

Don't feel intimidated or try to replicate someone else's work. Being true to yourself is always the best approach. A good example: After I had been approached to do the flowers for the Harrison Ford film *What Lies Beneath,* I was told that everything I designed would have to be exactly like what a designer in

L.A. would create for the set out there. I had been so excited about the prospect of working on a movie, but when I considered replicating someone else's work, I knew I would be unable to do it. Broken-hearted, I turned the job down. A couple of weeks later I received a phone call from the set decorator. She said that I could design what I wanted and they would replicate it in L.A. An incredible lesson.

I tell these stories in the hope that you will understand my ideas and how they can best be used in design. You don't have to become a professional, or design for any other purpose than to enrich your home and your family's life.

This book has allowed me to create displays of flowers based solely on the thoughts, ideas, and expressions of personality that I so want to share with you. I challenged myself to demonstrate the beauty and personality of a variety of flowers to help you understand that you can design quite simply as well as elaborately and be very successful. I worked with flowers I said I would never touch, flowers whose personalities I used to think brought out the worst in me. However, I have learned from my own rules that in combining some of the more intolerable varieties I could find new ways to express and describe character and personality. In the process, I actually came to like them. With flowers as with people, always give everyone a chance. Until you do, you will not know this person's potential! You may come to recognize that they too are just trying to express themselves with what they have to work with.

Over the years many doors have opened for me, and several others have closed. But with a tremendous amount of persistence and God's good grace I have come to this place in my life where I can honestly say I am living the life I have imagined. The life I have imagined is to share with you my love and passion for flowers and gardens and, perhaps, to encourage you to go confidently in the direction of your dreams.

CHAPTER 1

MY LIFELONG ROMANCE
WITH
FLOWERS

I am constantly being accused of being a die-hard romantic. It is true, I am afraid. Designing for me is still a very childlike process; I seem to relate to flowers with as much enthusiasm and curiosity as I did when I was a child.

When I was a little girl growing up on my grandparents' farm in upstate New York, I would spend hours outside playing in the fields, picking wildflowers and wandering around in my grandmother's garden. A tall stand of hollyhocks grew right in the center. You know the ones: single petals and dark burgundy. The petals were translucent when the sun shone on them just right. They reminded me of tissue paper, the kind in which bouquets come wrapped. The humming-birds, butterflies, and bees seemed as delighted with them as I was. Vegetables were planted to the back, front, and on both sides of the garden. For every row of vegetables there would be a row of flowers. Mounds of velvety pansies would call to me to pick them and hold their soft petals against my face. The bright-colored zinnias, placed in a mason jar, would find their way to the evening dinner table. This was my grandmother's garden, where the seeds for my future would be sown.

As tulips age, the most fascinating thing occurs. The outside of the flowers begins to fade and become quite pale, while the inside grows vibrant and bursts with color. Try to observe this sometime, especially with parrot tulips. You will be amazed at how the interior of the tulip deepens. I like to hope this is how I might age.

I had magical places on the farm that I visited daily. In one particular place three large rocks lay in a perfect semicircle on an outcropping up in the high pasture, as we referred to it. They had an opening to the east with enough space for me to fit perfectly inside. A piece of galvanized tin placed over the top created a shelter. This gave me my own little room with a wonderful view of the rolling hills and a safe haven from the Black Angus cattle feeding nearby. It was my thinking spot. Whenever I needed to get away and be by myself, this is where I would go. With the house in plain view I felt safe. I really had not ventured too far away, but since I had to enter the pasture and go beyond what I considered safe distances from the cows and horses, my thinking spot became an intriguing adventure to get to.

I remember one afternoon when, on our way home from foraging for wild mushrooms in the woods behind the pasture, my grandmother and I arrived at the top of a hill only to see two very large workhorses coming ever closer to look at what we were doing. As she ran by, chased by one of the horses, she called to me to run to the top of the rocks. I watched in horror as she dove under the barbed wire fence, mushrooms and colander flying in one direction and she in the other. Luckily she was unharmed, and all I had to do was figure out how to get off that rock and join her.

I was always thinking about ways to bring the outdoors in and decorate even small spaces like my thinking spot. My grandmother would supply me with old Campbell soup cans which she punctured with a nail on each side, pulling a string through the holes to make it easier for me to carry my flowers. Picking flowers found its way into my heart at a very early age. I seemed to be intrigued by their beauty; there was something about them that made me feel so happy.

The tulip stands tall in John Parkinson's *Garden of Pleasant Flowers* (1629), and his enthusiasm for it echoes the passion for the flower that gripped Holland in his day and led to Tulipomania, the first recorded speculative financial bubble.

But indeede, this flower, above many other, deserveth his true commendations and acceptance with all lovers of these beauties, both for the stately aspect, and for the admirable varieties of colours that daily doe arise in them, farre beyond all other plants that grow.

The French tulip 'Blushing Lady' gracefully arches and bends. Here chicken wire holds the stems so that they curve naturally, letting the personality of the flowers come through in the design. The soft green vase complements the delicate blossoms.

An unexpected pairing of two flowers that uniquely complement one another. The striking lady slipper orchid 'Maudie' with its distinct green veins mimics perfectly the slender green stems of the lily of the valley.

One of the most inspiring times of the year for me on the farm was in early spring: those days when the sun would shine so bright you could hear the snow melting from the roof, and finally begin to see the thawing earth. Every spring I would wait for the day when enough snow had melted from the fields to expose patches of earth where the first blossoms were waiting to spring forth. Although the woods around the house were made up primarily of hardwood, if you ventured far enough you would get into the softwood forest of thriving spruces and balsams. In this part of the forest, as the snow melted and the earth thawed, patches of what are often called spring beauties but I would call mayflowers, *Claytonia virginica*, blanketed the bare ground, looking like snow until you got close enough to them to see what they really were.

I couldn't wait until the mayflowers appeared. It meant spring had finally arrived and there would be no turning back toward winter. The mayflowers had delicate blossoms shaded in pinks, blues, and whites. The way they made me feel and the scent of the fresh earth from which they came called to me to pick them and re-create that lovely sight on the dinner table at home. I would pick large quantities, bring them home, and place them in mason jars on the kitchen table. For some reason, though, they did not make me feel the same way as they did in the field. So many stuffed into one container pressed against one another, their petals crushing, they barely resembled the way they looked in their natural setting—or any recognizable flower at all.

His mayflowers may not be the same as mine, but John Milton perfectly captured my feelings in his "Song of May Morning":

Now the bright morning-star, day's harbinger
Comes dancing from the East, and leads with her
The flowery May, who from her green lap throws
The yellow cowslip, and the pale primrose.
Hail, bounteous May, that dost inspire
Mirth, and youth, and warm desire:
Woods and groves are of thy dressing,
Hill and dale doth boast thy blessing.
Thus we salute thee with our early song,
And welcome thee, and wish thee long.

Flowers of just one kind placed in a clear glass vase offer a chance to enjoy the personalities of the flowers and their stems. Pink nerine, *Nerine bowdenii*, works well as a bouquet all on its own, and the white eucharist lily, *Eucharis amazonica*, in its own clear vase stands tall in the background, pouring forth its heavenly soft scent.

Determined to get it right, I began to cut out patches of mayflowers as they came up through the moss and transport these large clumps of soil and flowers home. Trying once again to re-create how they made me feel in the field, I placed them on trays on the dinner table. But instead of resembling a blanket of blossoms melded to look like a patch of snow, they were just long spindly flowers flopped this way and that. Not what I had expected at all. Discouraged, I returned the carved-out clumps of earth back into the spots from which they came. I would have to be content with observing them in nature. I was convinced I could never pick flowers and have them make me feel the same way they did in their natural setting. I thought that unless you were able to replicate what you saw in nature you would never be able to experience the wonderful feelings offered by flowers in such abundance and beauty.

From left to right: globe amaranth, *Gomphrena globosa*; candytuft, *Iberis crenata*; 'Yves Piaget' rose; white clematis; tweedia, *Tweedia caerulea*; pink astilbe

OPPOSITE: The peony-like effect of 'Yves Piaget' roses adds romance while scenting this sensual garden bouquet. Pinks, blues, and whites are combined in a way to accentuate the individual blossoms. A soft finish of white clematis twines around the stems.

flowers don't lie. They do not strive to be different. They work with all they have evolved and been given to attract what they need for their species to survive. The blossoms may be short-lived compared to the plant's life cycle, yet in this time they offer their bounty not just to bees and flies, hummingbirds and moths, but to us. We seldom ponder the actual purpose of flowers and tend, unthinkingly, to assume they are shaped a certain way to attract our attention and make us desire to display them to enhance our lives and living spaces. But those glorious shades of color, varieties of scent, unusual shapes and textures, the very things that appeal to us about flowers are actually created solely as a means of survival.

A striking bouquet of white parrot tulips; giant snowflakes, Leucojum aestivum; and lilies of the valley are designed as a hand-held bouquet tied with a handsome black and white striped satin ribbon.

A vintage basket overflowing with flowers for a Sunday service. This abundant collection represents a prolific garden and a thankful heart to our creator.

OPPOSITE: Everything in this arrangement was gathered from my field and garden: bee balm, echinacea, garden phlox, allium, delphinium, snapdragons, 'Yves Piaget' roses, hydrangea blossoms, and one of my favorites, Queen Anne's lace.

Bouquets began as delicate arrangements of flowers called nosegays or posies. The nosegay, dating from the sixteenth century, was just that: scented leaves and blossoms to make the nose gay. Ladies carried these diminutive bouquets to mask unpleasant odors when they walked in the streets of Europe. Men kept a handful of posies in their jacket pockets for the same purpose. These flowers and herbs were thought to have medicinal properties and would not only mask odors but also keep germs at bay.

A popular children's nursery rhyme, "Ring around the Rosy," which I recall singing in the school play yard, commemorates a deadly disease of the seventeenth century, the bubonic plague.

Ring around the rosy
A pocket full of posies
Ah-tishoo, ah-tishoo
We all fall down

The first line refers to the ringlike rash sufferers developed. The "pocket full of posies" is the little clutch of flowers. "Ah-tishoo, ah-tishoo" represents the sneezing, one of the first symptoms of the plague. And of course "we all fall down" refers to the succumbing of the victims. Luckily, today a posy is a charming collection of herbs and flowers given as a gift or an endearment.

My romance with flowers may have begun at an early age, but it wasn't until much later in life that I would find a way to use them to delight and inspire others. As I grew into my profession of designing with flowers, I came to realize that my experiences and observations as a child on the farm gave me insights that would help me communicate the life-giving joy and wonder flowers evoke in me. I learned that we should not attempt to re-create what God so masterfully designed but instead focus on conveying the feelings that flowers in a natural setting offer us. I realized that I could even feel anew the emotions I experienced on those spring days gathering mayflowers, which I thought I would never be able to feel unless in their presence. Learning to express and inspire an emotional response using flowers as my medium has become a way of life for me.

It is my hope that everyone who works with flowers will realize that these plants have individual personalities that can be composed to complement the characteristics of people or spaces. When you take the time to observe what nature is offering, you find the answers displayed in the flowers themselves through color, texture, shape, and form. You will be able to easily identify what types of flowers can be used to express someone's personality, enhance the decor of a room, or perhaps just offer a way of expressing gratitude or forgiveness.

Given the delight that flowers bring to me, what I enjoy most is giving them away: creating special bouquets for special people or special places. Flowers, after all, have been brought to houses of worship like churches, synagogues, and temples for centuries. My grandmother always brought flowers cut fresh from the garden to church in the summer. She would place them on the altar, perhaps to direct attention to the front of the church for worship, but mostly, I think, to thank the creator for all the joy and wonderment in his creations.

If you really look around when visiting a friend or loved one's home you will begin to see flowers everywhere—on fabrics, china, rugs, clothing. Consciously or not, flowers have been chosen to decorate the environment. I find it quite enjoyable, and instructive, to see what kinds of flowers have been chosen. It offers an enormous amount of information about the homeowner, some speculative, of course. How flowers are used and in what varieties, colors, and amounts are clues to a personality.

CHAPTER 2

FLOWER PERSONALITIES

one day i realized that i spend so much time alone in the garden or designing with flowers that i actually do relate to them and work with them as i would with human personalities.

Just like people, flowers display certain characteristics; and as with people, we are attracted to some and repelled by others. So much has to do with our own individual characteristics and taste.

When I ask students how certain flowers make them feel, the variation in answers is amazing. Take zinnias. One day while I was getting ready for a lecture I displayed in buckets on a large cart all the flowers I was going to design with. A woman happened to be passing by with her daughter. I heard the daughter say, "Mother, look at those zinnias, your favorite flowers! How they remind me of summer." Without looking up, the mother exclaimed, "They're sturdy."

The main philosophy behind my designs is to work with what nature has intended. Everyone who has been created has a place. No matter what their personality, they have something to offer that is unique. In relating to people you are always trying to build a team, whether it is in a working environment, with volunteers, or just for conversation and dinner. You want to combine the right personalities so that they complement one another and create an enjoyable experience for everyone. I have taken this concept and made it my approach to designing with flowers.

Stars of the cutting garden captured in an iron Victorian urn and supported by crumpled chicken wire. The vibrant colors and robust nature of zinnias explode with the joy of summer.

Some flowers are easy to work with. They can be placed in an arrangement and do not demand much attention. They just meld with other varieties, adding character and texture. These flowers I refer to as the peacemakers. Just like easygoing people, their presence is always welcome as they are so comforting and soothing. Then we have other kinds of flowers that demand a little more attention but still do not take over the entire arrangement and insist on standing alone. They have a gentle strength. Garden roses, peonies, ranunculus: with these flowers you can create an entire arrangement from a single variety, appealingly romantic, not overwhelming in texture, and not overpowering in color.

But some events need public speakers and dynamic personalities to get the job done, and sometimes you will need or choose to design using quite loud and dominating flowers. Remember that even the showiest of blooms needs support—not to take away its splendor but to enhance its already noticeable characteristics. Such flowers, which I refer to as Type A personality flowers, need to be the center of attention. But, like their human counterparts, it is all the support they have that brings out their best qualities.

Foliage, fronds, branches, seeds, and pods have endless expressive possibilities; they add texture, accent, and interest to the overall grouping. But they can also be real troublemakers when you place them in an arrangement, since they have definite minds of their own. They will twist, turn, and furl in the most interesting and unusual ways. They don't take direction very well. They resist manipulation and control and are quite happy to do whatever they want.

When working with the distinct personalities of flowers, try to relate even to the difficult ones with grace and candor. Never try to force a relationship. Trying to design with two kinds of very large showy flowers, for example, will meet with the same results as trying to put together two people seeking to be the center of attention. Flowers, like people, are wonderful to work with once you know how to relate to and handle their individuality and purpose.

When designing with a single type of flower in a variety of colors, it is very important to vary the stem length to add depth and character to the arrangement.

Sometimes beautiful arrangements happen without preplanning. Working with the oblong shape of the stone container, I put in chicken wire for support and then filled the urn with olive branches, nigella pods, 'Hot Chocolate' roses, and brunia, *Brunia albiflora*. This would appeal in any setting, from rustic to formal.

When I was in college I waited tables for several years to help with my expenses. Working as a waiter may be one of the most enriching ways to be really exposed to all sorts of people. The personalities you may encounter and the situations where you must think quickly on your feet help to build character in you. One evening, exasperated from having to deal with a very difficult patron, I asked the owner why she always gave me the difficult people. "Because you are so good with them," she said. I wasn't certain that was the answer I was looking for, but I did find out later in life that this quality would actually help me in dealing with flowers as well.

The domineering flowers screaming to be in the spotlight can be manipulated in a way to create a harmonious and pleasing arrangement. The way you work with difficult flowers should be very much the way you associate with difficult people. Let them think they are the center of attention, and don't take anything personally. Once you know what to do with them, you can put dominant flower types where you want them and they will blend nicely with other varieties of flowers and fillers.

When the tree peony is in season, it is one of my favorite flowers to use. A relatively easy plant to grow in zones 4 through 8, it has large saucer-size blossoms that are perfect for a springtime bouquet.

OPPOSITE: 'Karl Rosenfeld' peonies, white paphiopedilum orchids, lady's mantle, and a well-disguised yellow tree peony play against one another to create an airy bouquet. A soft gold double-sided satin ribbon adds a touch of sophistication. My newly arrived chicks look on, gently blending with their surroundings.

Texture is so important when designing—it is what gives a bouquet personality and substance. In my bouquet of tree peonies and 'Top' parrot tulips, the flowers echo each other not just in color but also in the textures of their fluid petals.

This is a perfect example of how I design and teach others. For this bouquet I looked into the center of a 'Savage Splendor' tree peony and, using the shading of red and cream, I chose a stunning French parrot tulip 'Top' in the same colors.

The Type A personality is sometimes considered one of the most difficult to deal with. Such people often charge ahead, determined to achieve their desires and dreams. It may seem like they just want to take over, but I think people often misinterpret their behavior as controlling or overbearing. I have been asked at my lectures if I have a Type A personality, and I am the first one to admit why someone would ask that. I respond by saying that I am perhaps less a Type A personality than an A+. My fervor and ambition may come across as Type A, but I assure you I could not be more genuine in wanting to share all this passion and enthusiasm. It is healthy, I believe, to laugh at oneself and see certain characteristics for what they are. Even those of us who are a bit more grandiose in our behavior really do want to be part of the team. Our need to be the center of attention and our talkative nature don't necessarily mean we are trying to take over. It is more that we have an enormous amount of energy and, as in my case, a need to share that energy with the world.

When I was in eighth grade I decided to try out for a part in the spring play, *The Wizard of Oz*. You guessed, of course, that I would try out for nothing less than the lead role of Dorothy. I worked so hard to learn my lines and practice my song, and I gave it all I had and then some at tryouts. The hard part was waiting for the decision. I remember the day they were going to post the casting call I had butterflies and anxiously approached the board to look at the roster. As I went down the list I couldn't believe what I saw: Lucinda Waterman: "Dorothy." I was so delighted I could hardly contain myself. A moment later, I felt a tap on my shoulder and turned around to find my drama teacher. He congratulated me for securing the part, adding, "Lucinda, you weren't the best, but you sure were the loudest!"

Now I want to become a little more specific and talk about how to design with Type A personality flowers. I call them that so you can have more fun creating with large showy blossoms and feel more comfortable about the design process. I can teach you how to work with these large and often stiff-stemmed flowers to make them fit into any design you want. With just a few simple procedures and ways to think about them, you can create beautiful arrangements with these dominant personalities.

There are some kinds of flowers that I have refused to design with until recently. Not necessarily because I didn't like them: I just couldn't figure out how to make them fit into the rest of an arrangement without being too overbearing. I decided to take my own advice and try some exotic and unusual varieties of flowers to see what I could come up with for this book. Working with large showy flowers can be a challenge, but when you deal with them in a more methodical manner you may find yourself laughing at how well relating them to human behavior helps in the design process.

A good example of this is an arrangement I decided to make using proteas, flowers belonging in the Proteaceae family, named after the Greek god Proteus because he had the ability to change his shape at will. There are many sizes and shapes of proteas, which are native to the higher regions of South Africa, with other members or genera in the family native to Australia. Their large bracts open to expose the flower within. Favored for their long vase life, protea arrangements are often found in grand hotel lobbies and restaurants. My first real introduction to them was in 1990, when I had an opportunity to work at the Chelsea Flower Show in London. While I was attending the international internship program at the Royal Botanic Gardens in Kew, I was asked by the British Bedding Plant Society to help plant up and maintain their display at the show that May. When visiting some of the other exhibits one afternoon I came upon enormous arrangements and displays of proteas. I had never had the privilege of seeing hundreds of these magnificent blooms all at once in a vast array of colors, shapes, and sizes: everything from king proteas, which can grow to measure 10 to 12 inches across, to the more refined pincushion varieties. I had never seen so many interesting and unusual varieties all from the same family. I was fascinated and have looked for a way to use them ever since.

I refer to the protea as a Type A personality flower. When allowed plenty of room to open and when combined with interesting textures to show them off, they work quite well in arrangements. Here *Leucadendron*; *Pieris japonica*; poppy pods; creeping club moss, *Lycopodium cernuum*; and leaves of the tropical fan palm, *Livistona*, set off king proteas. Proteas are known for their long vase life.

"The Indian Sun or the golden floure of Peru is a plant of such stature and tallness that in one Sommer being sown of seede in Aprill, it hath run up to the height of fourteen foot in my garden where one floure was in weight three pound and two ounces and cross overthwart the floure by measure sixteen inches broad."

—John Parkinson, seventeenth-century herbalist and botanist

Sunflowers: a Van Gogh painting, the end of long summer days, seeds to feed songbirds at our windowsills, and wonderful shades of burgundy, browns, rusts, and warm yellow.

When beginning an arrangement with large showy flowers like proteas, I find it best to decide first how many to use based on the size of the container they will go in. It is also important to adhere to one simple rule. If you have several strong personalities scheduled to speak at one engagement, you generally want to keep them separated. This applies just as well to designing with flowers. Place the largest blooms first and keep them apart from each other. Next I like to add what I refer to as my support flowers—something that gives interest and helps the A's stand out. After surrounding the proteas with, for example, a supply of poppy pods, I filled up the space, adding textures and colors to help bring out the hues in the blossoms but not to compete with them. The flowers I used were in shades of pinks, greens, and whites. So with that in mind I chose a *Leucadendron*, which is in the Proteaceae family; creeping club moss, *Lycopodium cernuum*; *Pieris japonica* branches; and two fronds from the tropical fan palm, *Livistona*, that back the arrangement nicely. This helped to bring out and accentuate the flowers and add a softer texture to what would otherwise be a very stiff arrangement.

There are ways to use several varieties of flowers that have very distinct characteristics all in one arrangement. When I was walking through the exotic section of the flower market collecting material, I came upon the most unusual and interesting flowers and foliage. Marveling at the intensity of color that tropical varieties display, I was drawn to a cut bromeliad with its vibrant red and periwinkle tips. The quizzical look of the tropical beehive ginger, *Zingiber spectabilis*, reflects nicely the wrapping of gold rope I tied on the stems. While the mini red calla lilies separate the strong colors, the exotic leaves pull everything together. I placed two dried cecropia leaves around the base of the coconut vase to add interest and to set off the arrangement. At first I was not sure that I could work successfully with flowers like this. But I have come to realize you can turn almost any kind of flower into a romantic display, full of personality. All you have to do is know how to treat them.

Cattails, tropical beehive ginger, calla lilies, bromeliads, and croton leaves form a contemporary-style bouquet wrapped with gold roping and set among cecropia leaves.

Type A personality arrangements are always popular at my lectures. Because I love to use people from the audience, everyone can enjoy my somewhat quirky observations and ways of relating flower personalities to design. To recall in more detail an experience I mentioned in my introduction, a man I had asked to join me on stage insisted on bringing his type A personality wife up front with him so that I could design an arrangement that looked like her in flowers. He seemed perplexed by her personality and made a point of saying that he was not certain I could design anything so difficult. So with his continuous assistance, as he explained his wife in detail, I began to design. I wove peach amaryllis with orange ranunculus and parrot tulips along with a soft enclosure of hellebores. I finished up the arrangement and handed it to his wife. He quickly removed the bouquet from her hands and decided to keep it for himself, commenting that he had never seen anything so beautiful. He realized that the bouquet looked just like his wife and that perhaps he had been overlooking some of her very important qualities. I sometimes wonder if I am a floral designer or a therapist! But I always love to watch the joy people feel when receiving flowers that reflect their own personalities.

ABOVE RIGHT: A sumptuous display of colors and textures combines flowers, leaves, seed heads, and artichokes in shades of peach, green, and brown. A five-inch frog set in a ceramic urn supports the lavish arrangement.

RIGHT: From left to right: butterfly milkweed, *Asclepius tuberosa*; smokebush; chocolate artichoke; *Leucodendron galpinii* cones; ranunculus; amaryllis; sandersonia; millet; fiddlehead fern; berzelia, *Berzelia lanuginosa*.

OPPOSITE: Gorgeous peach amaryllis are softened with salmon berzelia, orange *Asclepius*, and vibrant orange and green ranunculus.

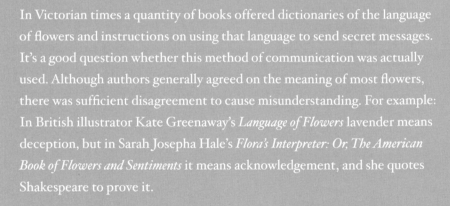

From left to right: green hellebore, 'Sweet Juliet' garden rose, mock orange.

RIGHT: Mock orange, *Philadelphus coronarius*, blooms along the walkway to my house, offering each visitor who stops to locate the source of such a perfume a moment of repose. In a bouquet it calls for simplicity and little competition from other scented flowers. Here mock orange is combined with 'Sweet Juliet' garden roses and papery green hellebore blossoms. The soft scent and voluptuous texture of the roses suggest an old-fashioned garden bouquet.

In Victorian times a quantity of books offered dictionaries of the language of flowers and instructions on using that language to send secret messages. It's a good question whether this method of communication was actually used. Although authors generally agreed on the meaning of most flowers, there was sufficient disagreement to cause misunderstanding. For example: In British illustrator Kate Greenaway's *Language of Flowers* lavender means deception, but in Sarah Josepha Hale's *Flora's Interpreter: Or, The American Book of Flowers and Sentiments* it means acknowledgement, and she quotes Shakespeare to prove it.

Also, the "few simple rules" were far from simple, and the confusion was compounded by a mistranslation from the pioneering and very popular French *Le langage des fleurs* of 1825. The first rule stated that a flower presented straight up (*présentée droit* in French) expressed one sentiment, and presented upside down (*renversée*) expressed the opposite. Unfortunately, an early English translator, Robert Tyas, thought *présentée droit* meant inclined to the right. Three sentences later the French says that inclined to the right means the pronoun "I" and inclined to the left means "you." Tyas seems oblivious to the contradiction and so do the British and American authors who repeatedly copied his *The Sentiment of Flowers* with or without acknowledgment.

Amaryllis flowers, with their large showy blossoms and long thick stems, fit into the type A category perfectly. (One thing to note, though: Amaryllis bruise easily!) Another way to use large showy flowers is to cut them down to size, then put them exactly where you want them. Controlling a controlling behavior is so much fun! After you place the main flower, it is easy to form the overall shape of the arrangement, adding the longest stems first and working your way down to flowers spilling over the urn like those in a Flemish painting. I love to let flowers do in an arrangement what they do in nature; this way the entire display will have more character.

CHAPTER 3

THE WAY I DESIGN

I really enjoy creating all kinds of arrangements: country, formal, sophisticated, simple, and sometimes just outrageous. Abundance is the key to expressive designs.

I tell audiences that less is not more, less is cheap. But I'm not talking about money or quantities of flowers. I believe that it takes an abundance of thought, passion, and creativity to convey in flowers the emotion you want to express.

One of my favorite ways to design is to make hand-held bouquets. Hand-held bouquets can take on many shapes and styles. It all depends on the types of flowers you use and how you shape the bouquet while forming it in your hand. My only suggestion for beginning the project is to have all the material you are going to use laid out in front of you on the table. Once you begin your bouquet, you will not be able to let go of it to clean more flowers.

Bursts of Blue Muffin viburnum berries sparkle amid bicolor 'Leonidas' roses and ruffled 'Bombay Pink' celosia for a lively mix of textures and shapes. A two-inch-wide brown velvet ribbon finishes the bouquet.

'Christom' Blue Muffin *viburnum dentatum*; celosia or cockscomb, *Celosia argentea cristata* 'Bombay Pink'; 'Leonidas' rose.

I like to start by gathering a stem of each kind of flower that is to go into the bouquet. Working with the more subtle textures first, I will lay one of each variety in my hand, crossing the stems over and turning the bouquet, adding more flowers as I go. People always ask me, "When do you know you are finished?" I always reply, "When my hand hurts." I build bouquets until my hand cannot hold any more flowers. This doesn't mean that the arrangement is too large, as I always keep in mind the person for whom I making it or the container it will go in. But I have found most really luscious bouquets are complete when I can no longer wrap my hand around the stems. When I have reached this point, I take a piece of raffia and tie off the bundle of stems. I will finish off the stems with ribbon if it is a bouquet to be carried, like a bride's bouquet.

Particularly if I am creating an arrangement for a pitcher or a difficult vase, I will make it in my hand first and tie the stems as I do for a bouquet to carry before I place it in the container. This way you can form a lovely shape and not lose it when it goes into the container. If I am placing the arrangement in a glass vase, I will use enough flowers so that they will stand on their own in the vase. However you decide to use it, the hand-held, hand-tied bouquet is one of the most pleasing and versatile ways to arrange flowers.

Poppies are one of my favorite flowers. Their papery petals and distinct centers cannot help but make even the most serious person smile. As happy and colorful as they are, though, they are not always the easiest to work with. I'm not going into the care and conditioning of flowers in this book; that's a book unto itself and there are several available. But one thing I will say about poppies: The less you handle them the better. When working with soft, delicate stems like those on Shirley poppies I have found that gathering several stems together and tying them before placing them in the container helps to keep the flowers from falling apart or becoming too damaged.

A sampling of the supplies I always keep on hand: half-inch green floral tape, wired twine, 30-gauge paddle wire, 26-gauge straight wire, spool of raffia, and dried kiwi vine.

ESSENTIAL SUPPLIES

Putting together arrangements and bouquets is so much more fun if you make sure ahead of time that you have all the necessary ingredients and supplies at hand. There is nothing more disenchanting than finding, when you have just constructed the perfect bouquet, that you have to put it down to try and locate wire or string. I like to check my inventory regularly to make sure I have everything I need before I begin a project. With a modest investment you can keep a supply of the materials you will need. These are what I generally use.

- **Raffia.** This is my preference for tying off bouquets. Raffia can be left natural or finished off with a ribbon.

- **Hemp twine.** Very sturdy and naturally cylindrical, this material can be bought in several sizes. It won't cut into flower stems easily and I like its looks just left plain on very casual bouquets. In addition, hemp is completely biodegradable—something we all need to keep in mind.

- **Floral tape.** Keep a good supply of floral tape. I keep half-inch floral tape, which comes in light green, dark green, brown, and white. I sometimes use it to tie off bouquets, particularly when I am wiring flowers and have to wrap the entire stem length of the bouquet to secure it before finishing it with ribbon.

- **Clear tape.** I also keep on hand quarter-inch clear tape, which is wonderful for making a grid over glass for arranging. Always remember to check your containers, though, after you have finished the arrangement to make sure none of the tape is showing. I will place the tape over the container in longer strips than needed until my flower arrangements and I reach our final destination. This makes for a more secure journey.

- **Wire.** Keep a supply of straight wire in several gauges on hand. Remember, the higher the gauge number, the smaller the wire. My favorites are 26-, 24-, and 22-gauge. I use mostly 26-gauge paddle wire for wreath making—it is light and easy to handle.

I also keep a supply of ropes and dried vines.

When I design I like to design as naturally as possible. For hand-tied bouquets, more formal arrangements, or simple displays of single flowers I use supports that offer natural movement to the flowers, as I have found these are the most pleasing to the eye. Chicken wire is a very handy resource to have on hand. Just cut a piece of the wire to the size you need, crumple it up, and place it in the container. For my poppy bouquet, I placed a piece of chicken wire in the bottom of the vase. Then I created small bouquets of poppies—approximately nine stems to a bundle—tied each with raffia, and set them in the chicken wire support in deep water. Not arranging them too much keeps them looking fresh and healthy.

Create individual bouquets of conditioned poppies and tie them gently with raffia. Arrange the bouquets in a container holding chicken wire and clean warm water.

OPPOSITE: Simple Shirley poppies, *Papaver rhoeas*, with their papery petals and contrasting centers, make an appealing bouquet. This collection in tones of red and pink is carefully arranged in chicken wire to allow the stems to bow naturally. Poppies of all kinds delight the eye.

TIPS & TRICKS
HANDLE WITH CARE

Poppies are so fragile that, once picked, they need extra care to keep them looking their best. The less you handle them the better. Singeing the end of a fresh-cut oriental poppy with a match will help keep the milky sap from sealing over the cut and preventing the uptake of water. I have also had great success by placing them in a bucket of very warm water, a bucket tall enough so just the top of the flowers reach over its tip. This keeps them standing straight and keeps the petals from being damaged.

Dahlias don't like to be handled a lot, either. If you pick them from the garden, make sure you do so early in the morning. Cut them with very sharp secateurs and place them in warm water. Add preservative to the water and change it every two to three days.

I.

II.

III.

IV.

V.

VI.

VII.

HOW TO
MAKE A SINGLE COLOR ARRANGEMENT

I. Texture is the key when working with a single color arrangement. Collecting an assortment of flowers with different textures allows each individual variety to stand out yet harmonize with the bouquet.

II. When you are creating a hand-tied bouquet, begin by gathering one stem of each kind of flower you are going to use in the bouquet and place the stems on the workspace in front of you. If you are right-handed, begin by laying a stem in the palm of the left hand.

III. Place subsequent stems over the previous one until you have one stem of each variety of flowers in your left hand.

IV. Rotate the stems as you add the remaining flowers to the bouquet.

V. Hold the bouquet in your hands and make sure it is large enough to fill the container you have chosen before tying it off.

VI. Loosely secure the finished bouquet with raffia and set it in a container filled with water.

VII. The completed hand-held bouquet, tied to maintain its shape, is then placed in a classic ironstone pitcher.

From left to right: white sweet pea, white milkweed, white dahlia, white clover.

In this book I used only frogs and chicken wire to support flower arrangements. I think the arrangements turn out to be much more natural and expressive when you use these materials. They are also environmentally friendly because you can just rinse them off and reuse them—nothing to throw away.

Antique flower frogs can be located rather easily. I find them on my outings to antique shows and flea markets. One of my favorites is a five-inch frog I found at an antique store several years ago and have used in numerous arrangements. The Internet is also an excellent resource in searching for hard-to-find or unusual frogs. Antique hairpin and wire frogs are very easy to use. Some shapes and styles are of particular help when you are working with longer and possibly more fragile stems. Antique wire cages also work very well, allowing you to structure the shape of your arrangement.

Finding inspiration to design isn't hard where I reside in rural Vermont. I could not live or work without the solitude and ever-changing landscape that is right outside my front door. When I visited Vermont at the age of sixteen I recognized that it was the place for me, and by twenty I had made my way there. Working hard for ten years—catering, selling my artwork, and designing flower arrangements and gardens—I eventually put myself through college. Now I live in a small, charming log cottage on the gentle slope of a hillside with a spectacular view of the Adirondacks to the west and the Green Mountains to the east. It is within this restful place that I compose my thoughts and create my designs.

My animals—cats, chickens, ducks, and rabbits—roam free, keeping me company and constantly delighting me. During the growing season I find myself wending my way to the gardens every day to sit among the flowers even if only for a short time, often for a cup of tea first thing in the morning. The birds are singing, the bees are buzzing, and my animals join me. They bring such peace, refreshing me to begin work with greater enthusiasm and inspiration.

'Casablanca' and 'Debutante' tulips loosely gathered and allowed to fall naturally form a graceful sheaf. Checkered taffeta ribbon finishes a ready-to-give bouquet.

Although I travel extensively for weddings and events, occasionally a bride and her mother will come to my home to discuss the flowers for an upcoming wedding or rehearsal dinner. I thoroughly enjoy these meetings as my little cottage helps to make them feel as relaxed as it does me. I bring this up to stress the importance of your environment in your ability to create and design. Whether you design professionally or just enjoy creating flower arrangements for your own home or work environment, to me nothing is more important than surrounding yourself with beauty. Even in my leanest times as a student or a single mother, I found, I can assure you, that beauty can be created without much effort or expense. Adding something that inspires you and evokes a creative spirit is essential in one's space. It isn't enough that we have an aspiration to design; we need continual inspiration to surround us on a daily basis.

Delicious burgundy dahlias combine with 'Tradescant' roses and viburnum berries to create a vivid effect in a collection of white porcelain and ironware. To support this arrangement, I placed chicken wire in the base of the white tureen before beginning.

RIGHT: Velvety burgundy dahlias, 'Tradescant' roses, and the berries of *Viburnum trilobum*, commonly called American highbush cranberry.

FAVORITE GARDEN FLOWERS

I always make sure I have these in my cutting garden:

- amaranths, *Amaranthus caudatus*
- blackberry lily, *Belamcanda chinensis*
- campanulas, *Campanula spp.*
- catmint or nepeta, *Nepeta mussinii* and *N. sibirica*
- Chinese forget-me-nots, *Cyanoglossom amabile*
- clematis, *Clematis* hybrids
- cosmos, *Cosmos bipinnatus*
- lavender, *Lavendula angustifolia* 'Hidcote',
- 'Munstead', 'Lady' (an annual flowering the first year from seed)
- peonies, *Paeonia lactiflora* and *P. suffruticosa* cultivars
- oriental poppy, *Papaver orientale*
- Shirley poppy, *Papaver rhoeas*
- purple top verbena, *Verbena bonariensis*
- roses, *Rosa* hybrids, garden cultivars
- salpiglossis, *Salpiglossis sinuata*
- sweet peas, *Lathyrus odorata*, antique varieties for color and scent
- zinnia, *Zinnia elegans*

No flower amid the garden fairer grows
Than the sweet lily of the lowly vale,
The queen of flowers.

Victorians welcomed John Keats's "queen of flowers" as a sign of spring's return. But the seventeenth-century herbalists valued it as a remedy. Just to mention a few of the "virtues" ascribed to it by John Gerard:

The Floures of the Valley Lillie distilled with wine, and drunk the quantitie of a spoonful, restoreth the speech unto those that have the dum palsie and that are falne into the Apoplexie, and is good against the gout and comforteth the heart.

The water of aforesaid doth strengthen the memorie that is weakened and diminished, it helpeth also the inflammation of the eies, being dropped thereinto.

A lily of the valley bouquet designed in memory of my dear grandmother. Simplicity and kindness conveyed.

Clients who come to my home for a meeting always seem to feel a bit disappointed when they arrive. For some reason, people think I live the way I design. They expect to see grand displays of floral arrangements decorating every nook and cranny of my cottage. Although I love my home and have decorated it to satisfy my need for beauty, grand displays of flowers are limited in their appeal. I live with flowers from my cutting garden when they are in season, and the rest of the year I buy them for special occasions. Or I may create arrangements when I have an abundance of flowers left over from an event.

I always seem to design much better when I have a purpose for the design. If I am designing for an event and not a person, there has to be something that inspires me to create. When I am having a dinner party or a special gathering at the house, I do go out of my way to share my enthusiasm for flowers. I decorate the house with arrangements and adorn the food trays. I love the thought of flowers with food. The two complement each other so nicely.

Creating arrangements with personality for your own home is one of the greatest ways to share yourself with other people. The arrangement does not need to be complicated to be expressive and interesting. I love creating monochromatic arrangements. A simple display of burgundy dahlias with viburnum berries and 'Tradescant' roses (one of David Austin's famous English Roses) makes an elegant addition to an all-white display of china. Something dramatic will catch the eye and quite often capture the heart. The textures of the flowers draw you in to look closer at their tapestry-like petals. The burgundy dahlias are so saturated with color that their petals look like black velvet, while the 'Tradescant' rose reminds me of Renaissance still-life

paintings spilling with garden roses simply laid in a vessel such as this.

I receive enormous inspiration and ideas for designs when I travel. Several years ago when I was visiting Paris I made it a point to wander into a different section of the city every day. Flowers were everywhere. Not only do Europeans shop daily for food, they almost always pick up a bouquet of flowers as well. I was overwhelmed by the beauty and sights, the romance and sincerity of Paris. Where else in the world can the sight of lovers along the Seine, street bistros, ancient buildings, and bouquets of flowers on every corner ignite such a passion for all the harmony and romance a city has to offer?

How beautiful the flower shops were there! Most markets carried bouquets or buckets of single stem flowers from which to choose. Bouquets were made up daily, each wrapped in a wisp of tissue paper just waiting for the right person to pick up on their way by. It seemed to me that sentiment was for sale, and that by taking just a little time to look one could easily choose flowers to match someone's personality. Another thing I noticed in Paris were the pots of lily of the valley in full bloom. They sold them everywhere in early May. I had seen them as cut flowers but never just growing in pots. I thought this would be a wonderful thing to do when I returned to Vermont. Forcing pots of lily of the valley in early spring, I would always remember that time in Paris.

Lily of the valley has been a favorite of mine since childhood. It reminds me so much of my grandmother. She was a strongly spiritual woman, and lily of the valley is said to represent purity and humility. To me it also represents the coming of spring, and patience, of which I had very little when I was young. I loved to pick lily of the valley with my grandmother. I would beg her relentlessly to come with me. I remember how tired my grandmother would get during the day. At about one in the afternoon she would say to me, "Lucinda, I'm going to lie down for fifteen minutes." Those fifteen minutes felt like all of eternity. In the middle of the day, I had too much to do and too many places to explore to even think about sleeping. Not understanding that my grandmother really needed this time to recapture some energy, I would create some sort of disturbance so she would rejoin me sooner on my day's adventures.

The bouquet I designed as a dedication to my grandmother is a simple hand-held one, made entirely of lily of the valley. Using only the green leaves and flowers creates such a pure and charming scented arrangement. It conveys her personality completely. The finely scented, delicate flowers bloom and bloom on their sturdy stems. The leaves with their arrowlike points wrap gracefully and gently around each spray of bells as if God intended for every bloom to be protected. Simply elegant, just like my grandmother.

You can make this bouquet the day before, as it holds up remarkably well. After I make one, I put it in a small glass of water, then in the refrigerator until I need it. This bouquet will hold up quite well even out of water. Once, when returning the next day to gather my props after a wedding, I found the bride's lily of the valley bouquet lying on a table with another arrangement. It had been out of water for some time, but it still looked surprisingly fresh. Lily of the valley is easy to wire as well. I have made lovely wreaths, boutonnieres, and nosegays with this delicate flower. But I only use this flower in season, as it is very expensive to buy in the market out of season.

CHAPTER 4

COLOR
AND
MORE COLOR

one of my favorite things in life is color. i live in technicolor, i dream in full color, and i have spent a lifetime observing and trying to understand color. color to me is the gift of seeing.

I do not try to be outrageous with color but to use nature as a guide. Nature has taken the guesswork out of color for you. She doesn't make mistakes in combining colors. By taking one single flower and looking at it carefully you will see color combinations that will work as well together as if you had used a color wheel. Haven't you noticed purple flowers with strong yellow centers? Looking closely at all the varying degrees and concentrations of hues in different individual flowers will help you gain the confidence to create more vibrant and expressive arrangements.

Dahlias come in a multitude of shapes, sizes, and colors. Mexican natives, they are usually grown in colder climates as annuals. My grandmother always grew dahlias, from the large "dinner plate" varieties to two-inch pompoms. I recall not being very interested in them as a child, but I have since come to appreciate them as a cut flower in arrangements. Still, they can be tricky to work when cut. They don't like to be handled a lot.

The pigment saturation in dahlias is vivid and dense. Many shades and forms in just the one color, orange, create a stunning arrangement.

A most useful technique that I have developed when teaching students how to determine a color palette for an arrangement is to have them observe all the colors and shades in one single flower. For example, if you look closely at the open and closed buds of a white lilac, you will see shades of white in the open buds, yellow green and darker green in the tightly closed buds. This one stem can be used to build an entire palette for a bouquet: white lilacs, Solomon's seal for the dark green, 'Lemon-Lime' amaryllis for the yellow green, white nerine for more white and airy texture, and white ranunculus to add strength and structure. Or, observe the mango calla lily. Look deep into the throat of this flower and you will see varying shades of peach, deep orange, dark burgundy, and yellow. From this I designed a bouquet with mango calla lilies, orange spray roses, lady's mantle, and, to add visual interest, purple clematis—a complementary color. Complementary colors create contrast and stability in an arrangement, pleasing to the eye and soothing to the soul—a bouquet of harmony.

Sometimes what we think of as more sophisticated flowers like calla lilies can seem intimidating to work with. I have found that even though it is a rigid flower you can shape both complex arrangements and simple stunning bouquets around it. Observation of the flower itself will, as I have said, give you clues about additions that will complement it nicely. For an arrangement of dramatic deep burgundy mini calla lilies, ringing the entire bouquet with a simple layer of hydrangeas gave it a more appealing personality than if I had used calla lilies alone. The very tip of the blossoms were a magnificent green, which I chose for the ribbon to bind the bouquet, giving it a luxurious look and a soft, romantic feel.

From left to right: lady's mantle, purple clematis, orange spray rose, mango calla lily.

OPPOSITE: I refer to this design as my Van Gogh bouquet. Why Van Gogh? Because he was a master at working with shades and hues of strong color. Purple clematis and mango calla lilies meld nicely with orange spray roses, added to create depth. Chartreuse lady's mantle softens the arrangement.

An arrangement of mini burgundy calla lilies and hydrangea that is truly simple to create. Begin by making a hand-held bouquet of just the calla lilies. Once you get to your desired size, rim the calla lilies with individual stems of the hydrangea. To complement the reds and pinks I tied the arrangement with a big bow of green double-sided satin ribbon.

From left to right: *Lavendula angustifolia* 'Munstead'; *Campanula latifolia* 'Brantwood'; Siberian catmint, *Nepeta siberica*; purple sweet pea; *Allium carinatum*.

OPPOSITE: Using several textures of flowers in the same color creates a vibrant monochromatic arrangement. Here campanulas, sweet peas, lavender, catmint, allium, and clematis blend together so well that the blossoms seem almost indistinguishable from one another.

Using several varieties of flowers all in a single color can create a beautiful arrangement. When making an entire bouquet with flowers of one color and little shade variation, it is important to consider the texture and character of the individual flowers. I filled a cream-colored pitcher with several varieties of flowers in shades of purple. For my arrangement I used lavender, campanula, nepeta, purple sweet peas, and alliums. This combination of bells, spires, and globes creates a fresh-looking bouquet. The cream pitcher complements the purples beautifully, and the bouquet looks as though I had just picked it from the garden.

I love to work with varying shades of a single-color flower and to teach my students how to do it. I have used as an example three different shades of gerbera daisies all in the orange and peach family. Even if you look closely, you can scarcely distinguish two of the colors, yet their subtle differences lend depth and character to the arrangement. Also you will notice that a number of the darker, more robust flowers have dark centers, which provide even more depth. The green centers of the other flowers pick up the color of the container itself and bring unity to the entire arrangement. Sometimes it seems as if you have to think about a lot when designing with color, but if you start with simple exercises like the gerbera daisy example, you will soon become comfortable with color relationships.

At first glance you may think that there are only two colors of gerbera daisies in this bouquet. Look closely and you will notice that three variations have been woven together to create a subtly cheerful effect.

When I look back at pictures of myself as a child on the farm, I realize I had very little knowledge of soothing color combinations. Although I loved the outdoors I insisted on wearing a dress every day of the week. Perhaps it made it easier to climb trees, but it was a bit of a nuisance when hanging upside down from a branch or swinging on the rope in the hayloft and falling into prickly fresh hay. No matter what color the dress, I would always wear my Keds Red Ball Jet sneakers. Those Red Ball Jets sure did help me accomplish a lot, and I did show up quite vividly in them. But when you design bouquets you are trying to put together flowers that work in harmony, and you don't want one to stick out from the rest. The point: Color can be quite jarring if it is not used properly in combination with other colors.

When I design bouquets using a lot of color I feel as though I am creating a painting with flowers. My favorite artists were masters at the massing of color: Van Gogh, Matisse, Monet, and Renoir, to name just a few. I find artists are very attuned to the effect light has on a subject. Since the color we see in flowers is actually the result of reflected light from various plant pigments, how they are lit determines how you will perceive their colors and the emotional impact they will have.

A good example of this occurred when I was working with the photographer of this book, Mick Hales. We used all natural light for the photographs here, so the colors you see are true to the flowers. One afternoon when we were shooting an arrangement I thought would be quite spectacular for the cover, Mick ever so politely disagreed with me. He shot it but explained to me that the lack of light on this rather dark arrangement of burgundies and oranges made the bouquet look flat and lacking in detail. Because I was quite happy with the combination, I was a little disheartened to hear this. Then several minutes later the light in another room was so magnificent that we moved and shot the arrangement quickly to capture the golden-hued light. Mick changed his mind and agreed that perhaps this could be used for the cover. The golden light had given the arrangement the aura of a romantic sunlit afternoon, which reminded me so much of a fall day spent in Provence a couple of years back. The important point: When you are designing with flowers, make sure you are working under good light. I use two all-spectrum 4-foot bulbs for this purpose when I don't have natural light so the true colors of the flowers are not distorted by unnatural lighting.

Spiky blue grape hyacinths, *Muscari armeniacum*, play off pouffy pink garden roses 'Yves Piaget' and 'Waltzertraum' in a vibrant contrast of color and form. The scent of the roses perfumes the entire bouquet. White organdy ribbon with a silver string tie adds a romantic finish.

To teach my son why leaves are green when he was little I explained it in this simple rhyme.

Light appears white, but this just isn't so
It's all the colors you see in the rainbow.
Plants use the colors red and blue
But that's not the colors of leaves to you.
It's the colors they don't use that are meant to be seen:
That's why all the leaves appear to be green.

Perhaps you want to design something as simple as an arrangement with one type of flower such as snapdragons. I was never that fond of snapdragons, but since I began teaching I have found them to be remarkable for their ability to demonstrate how a single flower can be used to combine colors. This gorgeous bouquet of snapdragons looks as if it might be all one color, but it is not. There are actually three distinctly different-colored flowers in it. I began with orange snapdragons, and if you look closely at them you will see hot pink and yellow on the lips and throat of the individual blossoms. I combined hot pink, orange, and yellow snapdragons and put them in a yellow vase to set them off nicely.

One color in particular fascinates me, the color green. Green in nature is so abundant that we often take it for granted. Spring is full of shades of green. Ireland is known for its green dales and forests. When I was studying at the Royal Botanic Gardens in Kew I became fascinated by the function of green in the plant world. I came to understand that the reason leaves and grass and so many things in the plant world appear green is that the chlorophyll in these plant parts produces food so that the plant can go on to flower and produce seeds. Plant life depends on green to manufacture food.

The colors found in this allium blossom—dark pink, white, and green—became the basis for a subtle spring bouquet. Double dark pink 'Daladier' tulips veined in green and white share the colors found in the allium yet lend a different texture to the arrangement. Lilies of the valley, with their gentle nodding bells and distinct green leaves, envelop the natural wrapped stems, awaiting a springtime wedding.

OPPOSITE: Fom left to right: 'Daladier' tulip, lily of the valley, *Allium siculum* (now called by taxonomists *Nectaroscordum siculum* and found in many bulb catalogues under that name).

Green goes with everything. As we observe in nature, it is the green of the stems, leaves, and flowers that sets off everything else around them. If you look really closely you will see that there are so many shades of green: blue green, yellow green, lime green. An exercise I have developed with my students when they come to Vermont to take classes is for them to create bouquets of harmony with greens only. I send them off into the fields to collect whatever they want that does not have a flower. This has proved to be a wonderful exercise, as they are able to capture the essence of a bouquet without being concerned which flower goes where. A couple of summers ago we had a particularly rainy season, and my design classes in July were met with some very hot and humid weather. When I sent students out to collect material for their all-green bouquets I wondered if they were going to survive the process. The mosquitoes were freshly hatched, and the students did a lot of dodging and swatting as they collected. But the arrangements they created were stunning. I was advised, though, that I might want to take before and after pictures—not of the flowers but of my students, who returned frazzled and bug-bitten from the experience.

All these variations of green work well when designing with flowers. In the flower-arranging world we usually refer to the greens added to an arrangement as "fillers." I prefer to keep these as natural as possible and head to the garden to find greens for my bouquets and arrangements. What I collect from the garden as filler will depend on the personality I am trying to express in my design. One of my favorites when it is in season is lady's mantle, *Achillea mollis*. Soft and feathery, the lime-green flowers brighten arrangements without being too overbearing in texture. Another green, which I use in substantial amounts, is Solomon's seal, both variegated and green. The variegated works well in softening arrangements, especially those of all-white blossoms. Since most of my arrangements are made up primarily of flowers, I do not use many greens other than those present on the flowers themselves.

There are actually three different-colored snapdragons—orange, pink, and hot pink—in this arrangement. If you look closely at the flowers you can see along the spine of the orange variety shades of hot pink and pink all in the one flower. That was the clue to making this three-color combination.

I'm very fond of green flowers, and bells of Ireland, *Molucella laevis*, is favorite annual in the cutting garden. A lime green calyx surrounds soft-scented white flowers, making a nice filler for bouquets and arrangements. It likes sun and well-drained soil, and it may need to be staked. The name is a little misleading, though: The flower did not originate in Ireland. A member of the mint family, it originated in western Asia near Turkey, Syria and the Caucasus. Linnaeus mistakenly named this species *Molucella* after the Molucca Islands in Indonesia, where he thought the plants originated.

Soft satin, textured velvet, cotton, and lace ribbons and gold cording are just a few luxurious choices to finish a special bouquet.

RIGHT: Gladioli are a summer treat in the cutting garden. Their unique personality and vibrant blossoms add character to any arrangement. Here I have combined simple red gladioli with a cornucopia of flowers and fillers. The neo-classical Italian urn overflows with sunflowers, sunflower pods, zinnias, dahlias, ranunculus, oats, grasses, asclepius pods, yellow crocosmia, and berries. The vintage French hand-loomed hemp linens still have the loom ties attached, which fall gracefully over the edge of the table.

Non-flower sources of color can also be important in making bouquets. For bouquets that will be carried, fine-quality ribbon is like the icing on the cake. Even when the ribbon doesn't readily show its quality, I can assure you it will be noticed by the person holding the bouquet. Playing with colors and textures of ribbon is a wonderful way to enhance a bouquet or gift basket. I buy expensive ribbons, but you don't always need to. It all depends on how you intend to use them. Some of my favorites are double-sided satin, taffeta, silk, velvet, and cotton. If I cannot find what I want, I make up the ribbon from a piece of fabric or vintage cloth. The choices are limitless. I also keep on hand a good assortment of roping and other trimmings, which can be found at upholstery or fabric stores. When I go to New York City I have fun poking around in the garment district, where there are many wonderful shops that carry these treasures at very reasonable prices.

Keep a good pair of scissors on hand, and label them For Ribbon Only. There is nothing more bothersome when you are hurriedly trying to finish up a bride's bouquet than a pair of scissors that have cut everything from wire to tape. In my case, I cannot blame anyone but myself for this problem as I have ruined countless pairs of scissors cutting what I shouldn't have when I was in a hurry.

CHAPTER 5

FINDING FLOWERS
AND
CONTAINERS

gardens surround my cottage and are a tremendous resource for me, not only for inspiration but also for blossoms and greens. Attracted by the colors and shapes and scents of flowers, I cloak my home with their beauty so that I always have the makings of a bouquet in my own frontyard.

What is more satisfying than going to the garden on a dew-kissed morning and picking fresh blossoms to bring into the house? This is a time to drink in nature and design anything you want to enjoy on the evening dinner table. Although I love and appreciate so many kinds of flowers, I do have favorites that I plant in profusion, among them several green and lime green ones: bells of Ireland, *Molucella laevis*; green hellebore, *Helleborus viridis*; lady's mantle, *Alchemilla mollis*; nicotiana, *Nicotiana x sanderae 'Lime Green'*.

A bucket of fresh-cut echinacea; *Alchemiila mollis; Achillea* 'Moonshine'; 'Goldflame' honeysuckle; zinnias; false forget-me-not or Siberian bugloss, *Brunnera macrophylla*; sweet Annie, *Artemisia annua*; catmint, *Nepeta siberica* 'Souvenir d' André Chaudron'.

An antique soapstone sink with crocks holding ranunculus, lady's mantle, safflower, garlic chives, and kangaroo paws ready to embellish the house.

The addition of interesting fillers will greatly enhance the feel of a bouquet. I prefer to access my gardens rather than buying fillers from my wholesale suppliers. Wonderful foliage can be cut from plants such as hosta, peonies, and both the common and the variegated Solomon's seal, *Polygonum commutatum*. And the soft chartreuse blossoms of lady's mantle will liven up even the subtlest arrangements. Such greens will bring the essence of the garden to the bouquet and give the entire arrangement a much more natural feel. If a garden is not available to you, there are still many things you can use in your arrangements: bay leaves, olive branches, rosemary, oregano. Many of these can be found at a local market or florist, or they can be ordered if you know you will need them for an event. I often go to the roadside to cut fillers for my arrangements. In the fall you can find all sorts of wonderful branches and berries. However, you must do it with some caution and take some preventive measures. First, make sure you are not cutting something that is an endangered species, a danger in foraging about the woods. Poison ivy can be a real hazard, so knowing what it looks like before your adventure is advisable. Also, make sure you are not cutting from your neighbor's yard or the property line. Even if you give owners the flowers, it doesn't make for very good relations.

For Nicholas Culpeper, another seventeenth-century herbalist, lady's mantle was "one of the most singular wound-herbs." It " is very proper," he says, "for those wounds that have inflammations, and is very effectual to stay bleeding, vomiting, fluxes of all sorts, bruises by falls or otherwise and helpeth ruptures; . . . the distilled water drank for 20 days together helpeth conception, and to retain the birth, if the woman do sometimes also sit in a bath made of the decoction of the herb."

A satin and velvet striped ribbon sets off a mixture of cheery 'Brandy' roses and chocolate cosmos.

Especially if you happen to live in the country, roadsides offer an abundance of material. Some of my arrangements that I feel have the most personality have been gathered from the roadside. I find myself scouting for possibilities when I am out for a ride on my bike or my Vespa, and memorizing the locations so I can return with my clippers. Hops, milkweed pods, goldenrod, asters, chamomile, chicory, grape vines, and yarrow are just a few you might meet. Do be careful, though, when adding flowers like goldenrod from the field or roadside, as some people who suffer from hay fever will not appreciate your gift. In fact it is best to find out before giving flowers if someone has any known allergies to them.

For this book, I cut large quantities of flowers from my own garden and bought a great deal from local growers. But I also traveled as far as Boston and New York to share with you some of the more sophisticated blossoms available only from a world market. I would gather myself together and leave home around one o'clock in the morning so I would arrive at the flower market just as it opened.

One morning in particular was an amazing adventure. On my way to the market in Boston I had to drive over a mountain pass to get onto the highway. When I was almost to the top of the pass I was met with a sign that said road closed. I thought, *How bad could this be?* Since I was all the way up the mountain and going a different direction would get me to the market quite late, I decided to take my chances and press on. On the other side of the mountain I realized just how bad it could be. I was traveling on what used to be a paved surface, but after washouts from torrential summer rains the road was carved away from the shoulders on both sides. I suddenly came to an abrupt stop: A young bull moose stood in the middle of the devastated road. He was not in any hurry, nor did he share my anxiety about the situation. Unable to maneuver around him I had to wait for him to heed my pleading and move on so that I could pass. Finally he decided to give me some berth and I proceeded down the mountain. Maneuvering around fallen trees and every so often losing the surface of the road altogether, I made my way to the bottom of that mountain. But I must say I gained a new appreciation for road closed signs and found an alternate route to return home.

Eventually I arrived right at 5:00 a.m. at the flower market as it opened. A bit bleary-eyed from the long night's drive, I was met as always with a bustling scene of color, scent, and textures. It is almost the same feeling I used to have watching Dorothy in *The Wizard of Oz* leave her house when it finally landed, only to find herself going from gray and black and white to colorful Munchkin Land. There is another world happening while you sleep, the world of flowers. Large carts pass by with towering boxes full of blossoms and foliage. People scramble from one vendor to the next to collect what they need for their shops and upcoming events. It's better than a double espresso latte.

'Black Beauty' roses and black pussy willows combine as a hand-held bouquet, which I placed in a small container inside a moss-lined wire basket.

A gaggle of geese scurrying from the camera cross in front of ranunculus, lady's mantle, safflower, garlic chives, and kangaroo paws gathered to arrange for a shot in the kitchen.

An undemanding bouquet of black-eyed Susans, *Rudbeckia hirta*, that I bought from a farm stand are formed into a hand-held bouquet and placed in a lime-stained, weathered terra-cotta vase.

OPPOSITE: A treasured potting bench located in my dining room acts as a buffet. The bottom shelf holds a collection of containers. Simple herb topiaries catch the southwest light and share the top shelf with a bouquet of black-eyed Susans.

My senses immediately ignite at the sight of the flowers and I find my way around the market pulling this and that for my arrangements. One thing I learned quickly about human behavior in the flower market is that you never put your flowers down while investigating another variety. If you do, I assure you they will not be there when you return. I don't know why people think the four bunches you picked from a container with several remaining must be better than those still in the container—but such is human nature.

Never before have I been given such liberty to design as with this book. Improvising as I filled my arms with flowers, I would scour the market for unusual and interesting material, trying to match the flowers to the type of personalities I wanted to evoke in my designs. Since some of the flowers I had planned on were unavailable, I had to quickly rethink my designs, which often meant using flowers I had never used before. In the end, the flowers just fit into my Subaru, leaving enough space to see out the side mirrors.

Think creatively, and almost anything that comes to hand can be made to display flowers well. Myriad items you may have around the house will do; from French galvanized flower buckets to fine china, there is always something available that can hold a lovely bouquet. Sometimes the quirkier the container, the more exciting even simple flower arrangements can be. In the spring I like scouring yard sales, where one man's trash can become another man's treasure. Sometimes I find the most interesting containers when I am not looking. I will come across appealing things that I buy and put away without a clue of what I am going to design in them. I know that at some point I will be inspired to create something with as much personality as the container it is to go in. The choice of a specific container definitely enhances the personality of a bouquet.

I always prefer natural materials to plastic so I look for containers made of glass, wire, metal, ceramic, grasses, and wood. Now, thanks to a more environment-friendly industry, there are rice-based containers that are biodegradable. For large weddings and events I prefer to use many different containers, all made from the same substance. If a wedding seems to call for arrangements in clear glass, for instance, I will scour flea markets and yard sales for suitable pieces.

Another item I use a lot is floral tack, available at floral and craft supply stores. It reminds me of Silly Putty but is much stickier. This is great to have on hand for securing plastic liners, frogs, and anything else that may need a little extra support. I will warn you, though, it does not necessarily take the place of tape. The tack will pull away from surfaces if the arrangement is too top heavy.

A selection of the containers that I have collected, from antique stores, lawn sales, European travels, and local artisans.

LEFT: A garden flower bouquet in an antique container labeled *Belle Jardinière Maison*. From the cutting garden, I collected gallardia, gloriosa daisy, bee balm, snapdragons, bupleurum, bells of Ireland, and nigella pods.

OUTDOOR & INDOOR FAVORITES

A few flowers and fillers that I enjoy growing in the cutting garden but that need space to roam:

- Gooseneck loosestrife, *Lysimachia clethroides*. This is a a hardy perennial easily grown in the home garden. Plant it where you don't mind it spreading, as it tends to take over.

- Nepeta, *Nepeta sibirica* 'Souvenir d'André Chaudron' is another good cutting flower. A member of the mint family, this plant blooms for a long time in the garden on 24- to 36-inch stems. It is a sturdy flower with just a faint scent that works well with other scented flowers.

- The 'Tradescant' rose, named after a famous seventeenth-century botanist, emits the heady perfume we expect from such a rich red rose. One of my favorites, David Austin garden roses, has blossoms that stay sturdy when cut and can be successfully grown in zones 4 through 9.

- *Bupleurum rotundifolium* 'Green Gold' is easily grown from seed and can be added to the garden as an annual cut flower for filler. Start in the spring indoors and plant out after danger of frost.

- Clematis is another flower that I keep in my garden to cut from. My personal favorites are *Clematis integrifolia* 'Roguchi' and *Clematis viticella* 'Polish Spirit'. I can successfully grow these varieties in Vermont both for their flowers and their ornamental seed heads.

- Gentians may sound exotic but many varieties can be grown successfully in zones 4 through 8. Two of my favorites are *Gentiana makioni* 'Royal Blue' and *Gentiana makioni* 'Marsha', for true blue lovers. Grow them in moist garden soil in sun to part shade.

A few flowers that thrive inside the home:

- The sweet-scented eucharist lily, *Eucharis grandiflora*, is a member of the amaryllis family. Also referred to as the Amazon lily, this tropical plant is easily grown in containers inside. Provide full to partial sun and moist soil. The flowers will bloom intermittently spring through fall.

- Scented geraniums fill my indoor window boxes in the winter months, their leaves ever ready to add texture and a hint of the garden long past the growing season. Some of my favorites are *Pelargonium* 'Red Flowered Rose' with rose-scented foliage; mint-scented rose geranium, *Pelargonium graveolens varigata*, for its wonderful variegated leaves; and *Pelargonium* 'Apricot'.

- *Jasminum* 'Ann Clements' is another favorite flowering plant to grow indoors. It grows hanging unobstructed in a south window in my loft. Its scented blossoms perfume my home from late fall to early spring.

This close-up of a rose crackle planter shows how effectively an unusual container enhances a garden rose arrangement.

LEFT: A garland created from wild flowers, berries, and branches embellishes a garden arbor to make an attractive entryway. Goldenrod; barberry; gray dogwood, *Cornus racemosa*; and maple seeds still attached to the branch were all woven together in this simple and satisfying project to make.

BELOW: Multiple bunches of collected material laid over one another make a thick, luscious swag. Forming individual bunches first makes construction easier. You will need quarter-inch rope or twine cut to the length you want the garland to be. Begin at one end with one bunch, tying each successive bunch securely to the rope with a continuous spool of wreath wire as you proceed. You can leave the garland in place to dry and enjoy it throughout the fall season.

RIGHT: It's harvest time in the garden—the best time to surprise a friend with a basket full of fresh-picked vegetables, baked goods, and, of course, a fresh bouquet of flowers. Zinnias, small sunflowers, gaillardia, ageratum, statice, veronica, and goldenrod fill this container to the delight of the receiver.

Plastic liners are often essential and frequently forgotten. If there is any doubt about water-tightness, always line your container so that you are not dismayed during or after dinner when you suddenly see a nice water ring on your cherry table left by your beautiful masterpiece. You can purchase liners, but a good supply of deli containers will do just fine and are a good way to recycle. When I need something even sturdier for a liner I cut down plastic milk jugs. These make excellent liners for taller vases that you cannot see through. Anything we can do to recycle and to use earth-friendly products will be greatly appreciated by our flowers and future.

Containers never need to be expensive. Often, I buy enough inexpensive ones to have some always on hand for gift giving. It is so enjoyable to add a fresh bouquet when you are making up a gift basket for a friend. What could be more delightful to receive than a gift basket waiting on your front step when you come home from work or an outing? The simplest of flower arrangements can give the greatest pleasure to someone, especially if you cut them fresh from your garden. Filling a basket with fresh herbs from the garden, a braid of garlic, fresh-baked Italian bread, and a mason jar with a country bouquet will definitely brighten someone's day.

CHAPTER 6

FOR THE BRIDE
AND
HER WEDDING

what is more romantic than a bride in a garden with flowers that speak so loudly of her personality you can imagine her genuine character just by the site and the composition of her bouquet?

When designing for brides it is a particularly good practice to observe and listen attentively during your meetings with them. I find it extremely helpful to notice what colors and kinds of flowers have been chosen for her surroundings when I am working with a client for a wedding. Also pay close attention to the color combinations the bride has chosen to wear, as these will be important in choosing the colors and textures of the flowers for her wedding. It is very difficult when designing flowers to convey to people what the finished results will look like, especially when you design on an individual basis. Sometimes this can leave your clients a little anxious about the event, so it is your responsibility to help put them at ease and give them confidence in your design ability.

A late-summer bride finds a dream setting for her wedding at Hildene, the historic Vermont estate of Robert Todd Lincoln. Heidi awaits her father beside the privet-hedged flowerbeds of the parterre garden overlooking the Green Mountains.

With flowers, as with many other things, beauty is in the eye of the beholder. The blossoms I find most alluring and pleasing may be disliked altogether by other people. The trick here is to not take offense at such rejection, but to use the information to guide you in making more pleasing arrangements for your clients or friends. When working with brides I find it easy to pick up on their personalities quite quickly just from the types of flowers they are showing me that they like. It is fascinating to work with them as they will either really love or really dislike a particular variety, with not much room in between for negotiation. From this I can compile lists of flowers and colors that will appeal to my clients just based on the personality they present to me. Being able to associate people's personalities with those of the flowers they choose will greatly increase your success in making others happy and confident that you are competent to create what they are seeking for their special occasion.

I have designed for so many personalities that I thought at least a few designs would be repeated somewhere along the way. However, I have discovered that all brides are unique individuals with varied likes and dislikes, especially when it comes to flowers. Quite often someone will arrive saying she knows exactly what she wants, when in fact this couldn't be further from the truth. It is so much fun to introduce flowers that a bride has never considered but that reflect her unique character and style and fit into the ideas she has developed for her wedding.

Polka dots and peonies are woven into this hand-tied bouquet to add charm and personality. A delicious blend of butter cream frosting and 'John Cabot' rose blossoms decorates a cake awaiting the couple to cut.

Since I like to design as naturally as possible, I usually make hand-held bouquets woven with natural stems, but I sometimes include wired flowers such as hydrangea blossoms, orchids, or stephanotis. If you are feeling very ambitious and the budget allows, another of my favorites is the all-wired bouquet, which I discuss in detail in Chapter 7, Getting Wired. Leave plenty of time to complete this type of bouquet, as everything must be thoroughly conditioned first. The wiring itself takes a considerable amount of time. If I am going to put the bouquet together in the morning I condition the flowers the day before and refrigerate them overnight. If I make the bouquet the night before the wedding, I place the bouquet in a sturdy glass container, mist it, put a large plastic bag over it and refrigerate it overnight. Either way, you will have the freshest possible bouquet.

The pink bouquets mix zinnias; pink sweet peas; pink snapdragons; catmint, *Nepeta mussinii*; and clematis 'Roguchi'. The personalities of these bouquets would suit children and mothers alike for a summer garden wedding.

OPPOSITE: Simplicity is the key in creating these diminutive nosegays. I like to take a bucket to the garden and make them right on the spot as I cut the flowers. I gather the flowers into a bouquet, tie them off with raffia, and condition them overnight in a bucket of nutrient-rich water. Full of color and charm, the blue bouquets combine bachelor buttons; borage; lady's mantle; swamp milkweed, *Asclepias incarnata*; 'Royal Blue' gentians, *Gentiana makioni*; and 'Strata' salvia, *Salvia farinacea*.

To give you a detailed explanation of how to create a bouquet that truly reflects the bride's personality, I will use Heidi, who generously agreed to model for my book, as my example. Heidi came to me last fall about designing flowers for her wedding, which was going to take place in August 2008 at a historic site in Vermont called Hildene. Knowing the setting she chose for her wedding already gave me a great deal of insight into Heidi's character and personality. Hildene was the estate of Robert Todd Lincoln and is located in the heart of the Green Mountains. From its pinnacle setting it overlooks the town below with a grand sweep of valleys and mountains in the distance. The estate is well maintained and its grounds beautifully manicured. When you go out the back of the mansion to the place where weddings are held, you step into an ornate parterre garden of clipped privet with seasonal perennial blooms. The garden is delightful throughout the year, but considering what would be in bloom during the wedding—the colors, textures, and foliage—was of great importance to creating arrangements that would look as though they were gathered from the garden itself.

Heidi is a naturally beautiful woman, gentle in nature and genuinely elegant. You could see that everything about her wedding was going to be authentic and executed with style and grace. I designed a bouquet that was simple and delicate in nature yet strong and graceful. Garden spray rose 'Lea Romantica'; rice flower, *Ozothamnus diosmifolius*; lavender larkspur; and wired pieces of purple hydrangea and green hellebore combined to evoke her style and personality.

BELOW: After an afternoon spent gathering flowers from the garden these two charming young ladies appear in matching cotton dresses carrying their flower-filled wire baskets.

RIGHT: Half hidden, my new kitten Henry looks on with curiosity at children's French blue wire baskets filled with flowers from the cutting garden: cosmos, zinnias, Queen Anne's lace, purpletop vervain, Chinese forget-me-not, and annual scabiosa, *Scabiosa atropurpurea*.

Field flowers overflow this antique child's watering can, which still works when it is tipped just right. Chicory; ox-eye daisy, *Chrysanthemum leucanthemum*; Queen Anne's lace; clover; and 'Cherry Jubilee' nasturtium picked fresh from the kitchen garden.

RIGHT: A country girl in a handmade dress constructed from vintage French hand-loomed hemp with cotton ties. Fresh-cut field flowers spill from her small watering can and posies adorn her antique straw hat.

I enjoy creating diminutive bouquets—for the bride's mother, flower girl baskets, or head wreaths. Going to the garden or field can produce some of the most beautiful and thoughtful arrangements, full of scent and personality. As a rule, I strive for abundance, but that does not mean the bouquet has to be expensive. I always have an ample supply of herbs in the garden to cut from: rosemary, sage, oregano, borage, lavender, just to name a few. When combined with the summer flowers that flourish in my cutting garden—such as clematis, salvias, bachelor buttons, sweet peas, echinacea, yarrow, and honeysuckle—and conditioned, they can form a romantic bouquet, one to be cherished.

For making flower girl bouquets I enjoy collecting unusual baskets and containers, and choose wire baskets over woven ones when I can find them. Interesting and unusual wire baskets lined in moss with containers placed inside are wonderful for either elaborate arrangements or simple fresh-picked flowers from the garden. The blue French wire baskets I used for my two lovely flower girls were purchased from a French antique store in Stowe, Vermont. The simple collection of flowers from fields and gardens includes cosmos; zinnias; purple top verbenas; scabiosa, *Scabiosa atropurpurea* 'Summer Sundae'; Queen Anne's lace; and Chinese forget-me-nots. (The latter is not a true forget-me-not, and when grown as an annual it will self sow.) The graceful blossoms have just the right character to complement the delicate metal daisies that adorn the handle. These arrangements convey the same purity and simplicity as my two wonderful models holding them. I treasure finds like these and so will those who carry them.

Another delightful container I came across on one of my outings was a small weathered watering can. I filled this with wildflowers and blossoms from the culinary garden, chicory, Queen Anne's lace, clover, nasturtium 'Cherries Jubilee', yarrow, and ox-eye daisy, *Chrysanthemum leucanthemum*. This collection of flowers fills the watering can with a delightful arrangement just right for small hands.

I have come to realize after so many years of design that almost everything I create is made up of bouquets in one arrangement or another. Flower girl head wreaths are a good example. They are composed of several small bouquets laced together to fit securely on the child's head. I enjoy creating the head wreaths to look freshly cut from the garden. I always make them the night before, conditioning the flowers ahead of time and refrigerating the finished wreath until it is needed.

I always keep oregano in the herb garden. Its minute flowers work wonderfully as filler in baskets and head wreaths. I plant two varieties: common oregano or pot marjoram, *Origanum vulgare*, whose blossoms are a pink/purple; and Greek oregano, *Origanum heracleoticum*, a culinary oregano whose blossoms are white. To make the sumptuous head wreath my young model is wearing you will need a collection of purple sweet peas, lavender sweet peas, green hellebore flowers, and common oregano flowers.

If you wove dandelions or daisies into wreaths for your head as a small child, you know the appeal of wreath-making and wreath-wearing. Wreaths worn around the head have a long history in plant symbolism. The Greeks crowned successful athletes with laurel wreaths; the Romans crowned successful generals with the same. Romans wore wreaths of parsley at banquets to ward off drunkenness! And in the Middle Ages a wreath of roses was the reward for virtue, first awarded, according to *Le langage des fleurs,* by Saint Médard in 532 to the young woman in his hometown of Salency who was voted by all her peers to be the most obedient, most modest, and most wise.

This young flower girl looks charming wearing a head wreath of spring flowers. Her soft curls and beautiful skin tone go nicely with the cool colors and freshness of the arrangement.

TOP: The key to successfully constructing a child's head wreath is to have the flowers you are going to use already formed into small bunches. Make sure any flower that needs wiring is wired before you begin the process. In my head wreath I have combined diminutive bouquets of lavender and purple sweet peas with wired green hellebores and oregano. I alternated the sweet peas and hellebores so that the wreath would feel more airy. This head wreath will remain beautiful if you mist it lightly and refrigerate it until needed.

ABOVE: In profile you can see how the head wreath fits snuggly, circling around the top of her forehead and dipping slightly at the back of her head.

HOW TO
MAKE A HEAD WREATH

I. Measure the circumference of the child's head going around her forehead to the center of the back of the head. This measurement is what you will want for the finished wreath.

II. Cut a piece of quarter-inch double-sided satin ribbon adding four inches to each end of the measured length so that you can tie the wreath off after placing it on her head.

III. Cut the green hellebore flowers from their stems and wire them. Cut the wires three inches long.

IV. Create several bunches of flowers no more than two and a half to three inches in length. Alternate bunches adding hellebore flowers and sweet peas. Be generous with fillers like oregano as this creates a full, glorious looking wreath. Example: For a twenty-two-inch wreath you will need about eighteen full bunches. I like to lay out all the bunches ahead of time so I don't have to stop to make more in the middle of wrapping the wreath.

V. Once you have all the bunches of flowers laid out on a work surface lay down the ribbon and, beginning four inches from its left end, start laying the bunches on the ribbon and wrapping each bunch securely to it with a continuous string of dental floss. Yes, that's right—dental floss! Why? It creates a much more malleable and lightweight wreath for the child to wear. Dental floss is also very strong so you do not have to worry about it breaking or coming apart. Continue the process until you reach the last four inches of ribbon. Tie off the floss and place the wreath on the child's head. Secure the wreath by tying the ribbons together and trimming them to look like a continuous loop of flowers.

LEFT: A gently draping bride's bouquet: White tulips, variegated Solomon's seal, white peony, 'The Pilgrim' garden rose, white astilbe.

ABOVE: Although most of the flowers in this bouquet came from the flower market, I always add seasonal elements to my work. Here I am cutting from a prolific patch of variegated Solomon's seal to bring together the white and green tones in the flowers.

RIGHT: From left to right : White tulip; white astilbe; variegated Solomon's seal, *Polygonatum odoratum variegatum*; white peony; 'The Pilgrim' garden rose.

CHAPTER 7

GETTING WIRED

Long before holders were created to hold them, bridal bouquets used to be meticulously contrived and wired.

I love the look of a wired bouquet, though I understand for the sake of convenience and cost it is not the most practical kind to make. However, I still want to include here the wired bouquet, in which the blossoms are all removed from the stems and fastened with floral wire and tape. Although most of the bouquets I enjoy designing are hand-tied, I have found ways to add in wired material when I want a more polished look or I want to separate single blossoms that would be too overpowering if I used the entire stem. I refer to the wired bouquet as the bouquet for personalities that need complete control. A wired bouquet is the only kind where the flowers may be manipulated to create any shape you want: waterfall or perfectly round.

Learning to wire will give you all kinds of options to create wonderful pieces like wreaths and head wreaths. It is a somewhat forgotten art yet is still taught at some of the most prestigious floral design schools in the world. Given some understanding of the conditioning of flowers, one can learn to use wire to create interesting and unusual designs.

This sinuous bouquet, stylishly presented in Simon Pearce glass, has the essence of sophistication in its simple lines and enchanting flowers. The natural drape of green amaranth tassels suggested a fluid composition with white cymbidium orchids wired in with individual blossoms taken from a stem of white phalaenopsis orchids. White gooseneck loosestrife, *Lysimachia clethroides*, and lady's mantle complete the hand-tied bouquet. Natural stems could be finished with a double-sided ivory satin ribbon if the bouquet were to be carried.

I have been teaching regularly over the past several years at Longwood Gardens and the New York Botanical Garden. Always trying to come up with new inspirational classes, I decided at one point to teach the art of the wired bouquet. I think my students were a little concerned about learning the wiring process in the time allowed, but what better way to practice this skill than to construct an entire bouquet? The example I made for them was a waterfall bouquet, one where the flowers are allowed to trail over and bend as they would naturally. I started constructing it long before my students arrived so I could put together a cascading display of flowers for them that, although it would cost more than most brides would ever consider paying, was nonetheless a lot of fun to create. I wove orchids, stephanotis, white sweet peas, gardenias, freesia, and ivy. We decided as a class that a bouquet like this would cost around $1,500. Talk about throwing money away! As I recall, at the end of the class my students were quite happy to have learned the art of wiring, but many were also quite weary and had sore fingers from the process.

From left to right: Wired smoky gladiolaus blossoms provide considerable structure to this simple bouquet of ranunculus, milkweed, and *Celosia spicata*, sometimes called flamingo feather. Peach 'Eden Romanica' garden roses and blackberries are rimmed with a simple whorl of lamb's-ears, *Stachys byzantina*. Delicate blossoms and sturdy pods of *Nigella damascena*, commonly referred to as love-in-a-mist, combine nicely with purple sweet peas and salvia.

It's fun to combine different selections of flowers that suggest the same personality but differ in their characteristics and color. In these three bouquets, presented in a sconce, I used garden flowers to give that just-picked look. Dusty rose, peach, and purple play well against one another, and the charm of these arrangements won't go unnoticed.

One of the most famous wired bouquets of our time must be the bouquet Princess Diana carried in her wedding to Prince Charles. This 42-inch-long by 15-inch-wide bouquet was composed of a variety of scented flowers and greens. As is traditional with wedding bouquets, a sprig of myrtle was included, snipped from Queen Victoria's garden. A total of three bouquets were made for the event: one for the rehearsal, one that was delivered to Buckingham Palace before the wedding for photographs, and one to await Diana at Saint Paul's Cathedral. Knowing how long it takes to create a bouquet of this stature, I must confess I cannot imagine having to create three of them!

Several kinds of flowers can be wired successfully if proper conditioning is done ahead of time. There are many books of instruction on how to condition flowers, and you should consult those for the kind of flowers you want to use. In the case of wiring, it is particularly important to make sure everything you are going to use in the bouquet has been conditioned properly. As I always tell my students, only wire excellent material. The shape it is in when you wire it will determine whether the bouquet will hold up or not. A notoriously difficult flower to condition and wire is the mophead hydrangea, *Hydrangea macrophylla*. I love to pull florets from the flower heads and wire them individually to add to bouquets and arrangements. I have had the best success with hydrangeas by beginning to condition them as soon as I receive them. I recut the stems, place them in a bucket deep enough so the heads just reach the top, and fill the bucket three-quarters full of nutrient-enriched water. I leave the hydrangeas to saturate overnight before I begin working with them and only work with strong stems and plump heads. Anything weak or wilting cannot be revived, and it will not hold up. Yes, there are sprays you can use, but I choose not to.

For some reason, whenever I teach or lecture, just the mention of hydrangea blossoms creates quite a reaction from my class or audience. A few years ago I had a very verbose woman at a lecture I was giving at Longwood Gardens. She insisted that there was no way to properly hydrate hydrangeas and make them work in wired arrangements. After offering an exhaustive explanation and sharing techniques that have been quite successful for me, I had to steer her away from the subject so as to get on with the lecture. I must admit I was a little tried by her persistence. I remember hoping she would not be in any of my upcoming classes. Well, needless to say, she had signed up for all of them!

It is important to remember when wiring that at whatever stage you wire the flower, this is the way it will remain in the bouquet. If you are trying to achieve a posy full of luscious blooms of open roses, for instance, make sure you wire the roses when they are fully open. It takes some pre-planning to get everything at the proper stage. Be careful before you begin to wire to have all your material looking the way you want it to appear in the finished bouquet.

Sunflowers, sunflower pods, and berzelia, *Berzelia lanuginosa*, burst forth from an aged terra-cotta container. The petal-like motif on the container resembles the sepals surrounding the sunflower seed head, which adds an interesting fillip to the arrangement.

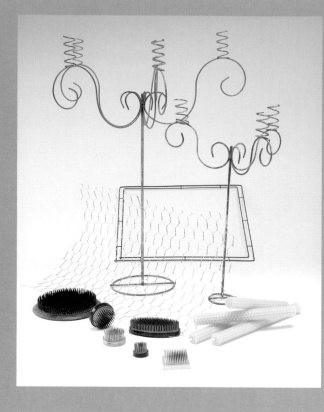

TIPS & TRICKS
YOUR TOOLS, YOUR CHOICE

Which type of floral scissors, cutters, knives, and pruners to use when working with flowers is a matter of personal preference. This is where you must do as I say and not as I do. I will confess to the numerous blades on my Felcos that I go through in a season because when I'm in a hurry I will use them to cut wire. It's much better to always have a pair of wire clutters on hand. I have a supply of them now and don't let them out of my sight. Needle nose, tin snips, and heavy-duty cutters will take care of all the projects I could possibly produce.

I always use #6 Felcos to cut flowers and greens. I know all the arguments that the repetitive motion and their weight may cause your wrists to develop problems. Again I believe that personal preference is what matters. I will caution you, though, that when you use a new pair of clippers with fresh blades, keep your fingers out of the way. I did a Christmas wedding once and while removing some greens from a garland I nearly removed my small finger as well. I have learned not to be so hasty in cutting and arranging material.

ABOVE LEFT: Wiring flowers to make them respond the way you would like in a bouquet or arrangement is easy. The basic technique, illustrated with gerbera daisies: Place a 24-gauge wire through the top of the stem at the base of the flower. Bend, allowing a long enough piece to wrap around the entire stem. Once the stem is wrapped, it is ready to arrange. The technique may vary somewhat for different kinds of flowers, but this is the basic idea. When it comes to cutting stems to arrange, my number #6 Felco pruners are my best friends.

ABOVE RIGHT: I made a point to design everything in this book with the environment and cost in mind, using an assortment of reusable frogs and chicken wire for all of my arrangements. I keep some interesting wire forms for wreaths, candelabra, and (not shown) topiary. All of these resources may be reused, and do not require a big investment. I also like to use natural beeswax candles. They are attractive, non-caustic, and actually help to clean the air rather than pollute it.

Wiring large flowers is an effective way to manipulate them so that they stay exactly the way you want them. Sunflowers are a good example. Instead of removing the head from the stem, I wire the entire stem. I begin by placing two sturdy lengths of wire through the base of the head where it attaches to the stem. I pull the wire about a third of the way through, bending it down and wrapping both pieces around the stem. This works very well for heads that want to flop down, or insist on not cooperating in the arrangement. An arrangement of wired flowers like sunflowers can look as natural as if you placed the stems without any type of control. Just be sure to honor the natural bent of the flower, and you will successfully create an authentic-looking arrangement.

You can find different gauges of wire at floral supply and craft stores for all your wiring needs. Remember that the smaller the gauge, the thicker the wire. Make sure you have a good supply of Band-Aids on hand, as it is inevitable you will end up piercing more than just your flowers.

Experiment with what works best for you and you will become very comfortable with the process. Once I have chosen and conditioned all the flowers I am going to use, I begin wiring on and laying out the bouquet. I do my entire wiring first, working on the sturdiest blossoms first and the more fragile last. It helps when you have completed a number of blossoms to refrigerate them until you need to work them into the bouquet. Once I have wired everything I need for the bouquet, I lay each variety of wired stems out on my worktable in front of me. Have your wire clippers and floral tape handy, because once you begin to form the bouquet it will be difficult, if not impossible, to put it down until you have completed the project. When you have woven all the flowers you wanted into the bouquet, you can cut the wire ends to a desired length. Then wrap them with floral tape and finish with an exquisite ribbon of your choice.

I mist the bouquet thoroughly and put it in a container with a weighted bottom, place a clear plastic bag over it, and refrigerate it until needed. I have had very good success creating wired bouquets the evening before weddings or special events. But I do keep them chilled until needed.

Three diminutive bouquets play with color and texture. The flowers have been cut from a stem of mini cymbidium spray orchids and wired individually along with pieces of green hydrangea. Each bouquet was designed with a different color of sweetheart roses to give contrast and interest.

The mix of flowers displays a variety of forms and textures: bee balm, *Monarda didyma*; bupleurum; orange butterfly weed, Asclepias tuberosa; green ivy; crocosmia; and 'Graham Thomas' roses.

LEFT: Ivy twists and twines around a wire candelabrum springing from a mound of mixed blossoms. Crushed stone fills a third of the decorative planter to hold the wire form upright and to add extra weight so that the arrangement won't tumble over in the wind if it is used outside. Chicken wire packed securely around the form supports the flowers to make an alluring arrangement that would be welcome on any table setting.

A simple bouquet of white phalaenopsis orchids, dendrobium orchid blossoms, gooseneck loosestrife, lady's mantle, and draping green amaranth tassels come together to form a cascading arrangement any bride would love to carry. The personality of this bouquet is slightly sophisticated, with some softer elements like the loosestrife and lady's mantle. Only the orchids are wired into the bouquet; everything else is left with natural stems.

Other blossoms that lend themselves to wiring are those of gladioli. I have always been a little unsure about the gladiolus. If I had to put a personality on the flower, I think of it as solemn or quite rigid. However, since working with them for my book I have gained a greater appreciation for gladioli. I am uncertain where my apprehensive feelings toward them started, since my grandmother always planted several rows of them in the garden. It probably wasn't until later in life that I began to view them with some reserve. Gladioli are actually quite pleasant flowers. They bloom for a long time and are remarkably sturdy to wire. I incorporated the blossoms of rose pink gladiolus into my bouquet with pinks and mauves (page 138). The flowers hold up extremely well and I have a new respect for them.

Mini cymbidium orchid blossoms are another of my favorite flowers to wire and add to bouquets (page 144). Pulling the delicate blossoms from the stem, I wire them with two pieces of thin wire and get them ready to weave into my bouquet. With pieces of wired hydrangea and roses they create a delightful nosegay that will stay fresh and lively-looking all day. These are good options for bridesmaids or mothers who may want something to carry but refuse the traditional corsage. I don't blame them. I am partial to these delightful bouquets as well.

Wreath-making for me is definitely a fall practice. With little time to make things for my home during the summer months, I look forward to autumn, when I can enjoy making wreaths for the holidays. I love all shapes and sizes of wreaths, but I am particular fond of the square wreath. I find its handsome shape is a must for my front door by the beginning of October.

To make such a wreath you will need a square wreath form. The one I used for this project was a fourteen-inch wire form. I like to wrap the form with moss if it is available. If the wreath is hanging on the front door and the back is visible from the inside, it is more pleasing to look at moss than wire. I begin my wreath project just as I do all my wiring projects. I lay out all the materials I will need on the table, so that once I begin the project I will not have to scramble for anything. I make all the individual bunches up beforehand and have them all laid out on the table as well. For a fourteen-inch wreath I plan on using approximately twenty bunches of four-inch material. Be generous, as the more bunches you add, the fuller your wreath will be when it is finished.

White cymbidium and phalaenopsis orchids, gooseneck loosestrife, lady's mantle, green amaranthus, *Amaranthus caudatus.*

For my wreath project I used rosehips and 'Golden Drumstick' craspedia, *Craspedia globosa*. I left the yellow-colored leaves on the hips; although these would not have looked healthy in an arrangement, for my wreath they added just the right amount of natural fall color to help the rosehips and craspedia stand out. Beginning at the upper left corner of the wreath form I placed my first bundle, using 26-gauge paddle wire to secure it. I continued placing the bundles one over the other until the entire wreath form was covered, making sure all the stem ends were securely tied and invisible. For a wreath with such heavy berries I usually lay the finished wreath on a flat surface to dry a little for a few days and then hang it on the door. That way berries won't be pulled down by gravity and will look much more natural when hanging. If you want to include fruit or other very heavy items that don't have stems, it is essential to have an assortment of bamboo skewers on hand. I buy several lengths and thicknesses of skewers and keep a supply in my workbag.

OPPOSITE: Rosehips and golden drumsticks bunched together create a luscious wreath. The unusual square shape is a refreshing change from the common circle. An inexpensive project, wreath making is a good use for even the simplest of materials. This square wreath is particularly effective against the rough stucco wall.

BELOW: Constructing a wreath is both easy and gratifying. After you decide on the material you would like to include in the wreath, begin by creating enough bunches of your material so that you don't have to stop once you start. Here I used rosehips and 'Golden Drumstick' craspedia, *Craspedia globosa*.

Whether they are in the form of spheres, baskets, or candelabra, I enjoy creating arrangements for the dinner table or parties with wire forms. How romantic it is when you add candles and flowers to the dinner table! Any hostess will greatly appreciate you arriving with a gift so appropriate for the occasion. All kinds of wire forms are available, but one of my favorites is a three-branch candelabrum made of galvanized wire, which I buy from one of my suppliers. I put the form in a sturdy waterproof pot one-third full of cleaned crushed stone to weight it. Packing chicken wire around the form, I fill the container with water before I begin adding the flowers. For this arrangement I used 'Michelangelo' garden roses, crocosmia, bupleurum, bee balm, and butterfly weed, *Asclepias tuberosa*.

Blue hydrangea, *Hydrangea macrophylla*, wired in with orange Mokara orchids make a simple yet striking Elizabethan-style bouquet. The stems are wrapped with salmon double-sided satin ribbon and laced with peach seam binding. Delicate in nature, this bouquet signifies a fervent personality.

Addison Gardens
www.addisongardens.com
Excellent website for researching unusual plant material. Paul Sokol offers a wealth of horticultural information and advice.

Alpine Home
618 South Main Street
Stowe, Vermont 05672
(802) 253-7005
Country French antiques—très bien!

April Cornell
P.O. Box 588
Burlington, Vermont 05402
(888) 332-7745
www.aprilcornell.com
Ladies' and girls' dresses, accessories, home décor, and gifts.

Belladonna
51 Main Street
Middlebury, Vermont 05753
(802) 388-4446
Antiques; an eclectic assortment of furnishings and collectibles.

Baker Creek Heirloom Seeds
2278 Baker Creek Road
Mansfield, Missouri 65704
(417) 924-8917
www.rareseeds.com
Heirloom seeds, wonderful selection of unusual and interesting varieties.

Cady's Falls Nursery
637 Duhamel Road
Morrisville, Vermont 05661
(802) 888-5559
www.cadysfallsnursery.com
Herbaceous perennials and woody plants for northern gardens. Growing rare and unusual varieties. One of the best nurseries in the Northeast.

Campo de' Fiori
www.campodefiori.com
1815 North Main Street, Route 7
Sheffield, Massachusetts 01257
(413) 528-1857
Garden and retail store. Aged, mossed terra-cotta planters.

Chalk Hill Clematis
P.O. Box 1847
Healdsburg, California 95448
(707) 433-8416
www.chalkhillclematis.com
Clematis cut flower grower.

Chester Brown Wholesale Florist Inc.
540 Albany Street
Boston, Massachusetts 02118
(617) 426-0943
Flowers to the trade only.

Christos Bridal
www.christosbridal.com
Wedding dresses.

Dorothy Biddle
348 Greeley Lake Road
Greeley, Pennsylvania 18425
(570) 226-3239
www.dorothybiddle.com
Floral supplies.

Eyeltalia Linen
1001 Bridgeway, Suite 533
Sausalito, California 94965
www.eyeltalia.com
Luxury Italian textiles.

Foote Street Farm Stand
2571 Route 7 South
Middlebury, VT 05753
(802) 398-2052
Cut flowers, organic feed, and home-baked goods.

Garden Valley Ranch
498 Pepper Road
Petaluma, California 94952
(707) 795-0919
www.gardennvalleyranch.com
A wide variety of garden roses.

G. Page Wholesale Flowers
120 West 28th Street
New York, New York 10001
(212) 741-8928
www.gpage.com
A wide range of high-quality cut flowers. To the trade only.

Green Mountain Florist Supply
45 Swift Street
South Burlington, Vermont 05401
(800) 639-7077
www.gmfsi.com
Flowers to the trade only.

Hallock Hill Farms Greenhouse
Route 7
Brandon, Vermont 05733
(802) 247-6630; (802) 877-2410
Kelly Sweeney, kellysweeney@together.net
Unusual varieties of flowering annuals, vines, and perennials. A collection of interesting pots and garden décor.

Hedstrom & Judd
401 Warren Street
Hudson, New York
(518) 671-6131
www.hedstrom-judd.com
Old and new botanicals, furniture, linens, beds, ceramics, and lighting.

Herrera Ornamental Iron Works, Inc.
2802 Oak Springs Drive
Austin, Texas 78702
(512) 926-5555
www.herreraironworks.com
Ornamental ironwork, custom designs.
This is by far my favorite artisan for custom ironwork for the home and garden.

Hyman Hendler & Sons Ribbons
21 West 38th Street
New York, New York 10018
(212) 840-8393
www.hymanhendler.com
Sumptuous, authentic ribbons.

Kelley Wholesale Florist
540 Albany Street
Boston, Massachusetts 02215
(800) 423-4238; (617) 423-5896
www.kelleywholesale.com
Flowers to the trade only.

Maine Wreath Company
P.O. Box 515
Newport, Maine 04953
(877) 846-3797
www.mainewreathco.com
Wonderful assortment of wreath forms, including hard-to-find square wreath forms.

McMurray Hatchery
(800) 456-3280
www.mcmurrayhatchery.com
The world's largest rare-breed hatchery.

Midori, Inc.
708 Sixth Avenue North
Seattle, Washington 98109
(800) 659-3049
www.midoriribbon.com
Fine ribbons and papers.

Nicole Maleine Antiques, Inc.
121 North Goldthwaite Street
Montgomery, Alabama 36104
www.tias.com/stores/nma
Fine French antiques and accessories.

Murray Rosen
Healdsburg, California
(707) 431-2730; (707) 228-9447
Murray-rosen@sbcglobal.net
Clematis specialist, floriculture consulting.

Patina
5288 Shelburne Road
Shelburne, Vermont 05482
(802) 985-5609
Authentic European furniture, antiques, reconstructions, and unusual paint finishes.

Periwinklebloom
www.periwinklebloom.com
Products homegrown and handcrafted in the U.S. using linen, cotton, and paper.

Renee's Garden Seeds
www.reneesgarden.com
Excellent selection of cut flower, gourmet vegetable, and kitchen herb seeds.

Rocky Dale Gardens
806 Rockydale Road
Bristol, Vermont 05443
www.rockydalegardens.com
Beautiful nursery and gardens set in the hills of Vermont.

Seeds of Change
www.seedsofchange.com
Certified organic seed. Unusual and hard-to-find varieties for vegetable and flower garden.

Simon Pearce Glass
(800) 774-5277
www.simonpearce.com
Hand-blown vases, glasses, and specialty items.

The Gilded Cage
58 Main Street
Middlebury, Vermont 05753
(802) 388-4442
Cynthia C. Pratt
thegildedcagevt@yahoo.com
Vintage antiques and inspiration for any décor.

The Perfect Image
6800 Route 7
Brandon, Vermont 05733
(802) 353-1513
Antiques, collectibles, and custom mirrored windows.

The Vermont Wreath Company
Route 7
Danby, Vermont 05739
(802) 293-5333
www.vermontwreath.com
Antiques.

The Textile Trunk
www.textiletrunk.com
My favorite source for authentic French fabrics. Hundred-year-old bolts of hemp and linen cloth, rare and hard-to-find prints, and grain sacks.

Topiary Inc.
4520 West Watrous Avenue
Tampa, Florida 33629
(813) 286-8626; (813) 839-1547
www.topiaryinc.com.
Topiary wire forms, wire candelabra, wire rings, and hoops for training vines.

Vermont Honey Lights
9 Main Street
Bristol, Vermont 05443
(800) 322-2660; (802) 453-3952
www.vermonthoneylights.com.
Authentic beeswax candles, antiques, and old world furnishings.

Wood's Market Gardens and Farm Stand
Route 7
Brandon, Vermont 05733
(802) 247-6630
www.woodsmarketgarden.com.
Annuals and perennials.

ACKNOWLEDGMENTS

In the past, when I have read the acknowledgments in books, I have often wondered how that many people could possibly have been involved in a single project. Now, considering the book before you, I am humbled and greatly appreciative to all those who have given their inspiration, talent, encouragement, support, and endless hours of creative labor to see this project through to completion. To all of them I give my deepest and most sincere gratitude.

Denise Otis, who not only edited and contributed to this manuscript, but so eloquently sorted me out. Not an easy task for anyone to accomplish, I assure you!

Leslie Stoker, my publisher; Jennifer Levesque and Kate Norment, my editors at STC; Alissa Faden, my designer, and all those at Stewart, Tabori and Chang who have believed in this project and have brought it to fruition. Their enthusiasm and great sense of style have created a very beautiful book.

Gale Hurd, a special friend, who graciously bestowed funds that helped me purchase materials and made life a little easier so I could focus on this project.

To the many nurseries, shopkeepers, and purveyors—especially Kelley Sweeney, Cindy Pratt, Wendy Lewis, Rachael Teachout, Tyler Stallings, and April Cornell—who let me borrow more than I should have to add authenticity and style to my bouquets and designs.

Mary and Ian for letting me shoot in their very special garden.

Mick Hales and his wife, Christine, for all their enthusiasm about the project. I thank Mick, whose work graces the pages of this book, for his unyielding artistic expression of my work through photography.

My young models Amber, Haley, Innogen, and Emily, who modeled patiently in my gardens, sometimes with a late afternoon flush of mosquitoes that made the job that much harder.

Heidi VanEvera, who modeled as my bride, and authentically stood in the garden at Hildene just one month before marrying (for real) Brad, the love of her life.

Hildene and friends for the use of the historic estate of Robert Todd Lincoln in Manchester, Vermont.

Leslie Fuller for her expertise in makeup for all my models.

The Weybridge Congregational Church for allowing me to use this quintessential New England landmark as a backdrop for one of my bouquets.

Lauren Page, from G. Page Wholesale Flowers in New York City, who tirelessly helped to identify varieties of flowers to make sure everything would be labeled correctly.

Paul Sokol, Ed Burke, and John Wood of Addison Gardens, Rockydale, and Wood's Market, respectively, for all the expert horticultural advice and plant identification.

My ducks, geese, cats, and baby chicks who responded well to morsels and coaxing in exchange for the perfect shot.

And, last but not least, my dear son, Isaac, and his father, Jon Rooney, for all their support through the changing schedules, travel, and preparation for shoots that sometimes kept me occupied for hours on end. And to Isaac for his eye and his aesthetic opinions, which helped me when I had questions about color combinations or the appearance of some of my arrangements.

INDEX